RELIGION
AND THE
AMERICAN DREAM

RELIGION AND THE AMERICAN DREAM

The Search for Freedom
Under God

By
CHRISTOPHER F. MOONEY, S.J.

THE WESTMINSTER PRESS
Philadelphia

Book Design by Dorothy Alden Smith

Published by The Westminster Press®
Philadelphia, Pennsylvania

PRINTED IN THE UNITED STATES OF AMERICA

Library of Congress Cataloging in Publication Data

Mooney, Christopher F   1925–
    Religion and the American dream.

    First presented as the Bicentennial Lectures at St. Joseph's College, Philadelphia, 1975–1976.
    Includes bibliographical references.
    1. United States—Religion—Addresses, essays, lectures. 2. Church and state in the United States—Addresses, essays, lectures. 3. Justice—Addresses, essays, lectures. 4. Liberty—Addresses, essays, lectures. I. Title.
BR516.M66   261.8'0973   76–54332
ISBN 0–664–24135–2

To Ce and Dick
  who have become family for me

CONTENTS

PREFACE

Chapters of this book were first presented as the Bicentennial Lectures at St. Joseph's College, Philadelphia, where I spent the 1975–1976 academic year as visiting professor of theology. Reactions of listeners there and at other institutions as well as the criticism of thoughtful readers have resulted in some changes and additions in the original text, but essentially Chapters 1–4 are the same as originally delivered. In preparing the manuscript for publication, I added an Introduction and a Conclusion.

I wish to thank those who invited me to deliver these lectures and all who made my stay at St. Joseph's College such a rewarding experience, especially Terrence Toland, S.J., President; Thomas P. Melady, Executive Vice-President; and Eugene McCreesh, S.J., Superior of the Jesuit Community. Special gratitude is due to Martin Tripole, S.J., Margaret A. Farley, R.S.M., and Richard Mooney, who offered valuable suggestions and criticism; to Helen Zeccola, who proofread the entire manuscript; and to Eva Steiner, who typed the original material with accuracy and patience.

C.F.M.

INTRODUCTION

The theme I follow in this book was initially suggested to me by a passage from Edmund Burke's *Reflections on the Revolution in France:* "To make a government requires no great prudence. Settle the seat of power, teach obedience and the work is done. To give freedom is still more easy. It is not necessary to guide, it only requires to let go the rein. But to form a *free Government,* that is to temper together these opposite elements of liberty and restraint in one consistent work requires much thought, deep reflection, a sagacious, powerful and combining mind."[1] I was struck by the fact that Burke omits mention of that third element which all free governments in the West have had to grapple with, and which has sufficiently complicated every attempt to combine liberty and restraint in the public forum, namely, religion. The power and force of religious conviction in civil affairs is scarcely to be underestimated. In Chapter 1, I recall what Mark Twain once said: religion is pretty dangerous stuff if you get it wrong. At a recent conference on religious liberty, Robert McAfee Brown reminded me of this once again when he quoted an anonymous seventeenth-century writer: "I had rather see coming toward me a whole regiment with drawn swords, than one lone Calvinist convinced that he is doing the will of God." Religiously committed persons will have little difficulty applying this to their own particular tradition, whether Protestant, Jewish, or Roman Catholic.

What I have attempted, then, is an evaluation of some of the public consequences stemming from the fact that freedom in America has been experienced historically as freedom under God as well as under law. Unlike absolutist monarchies or so-called totalitarian democracies, which minutely regulate in one way or another almost every aspect of church activity, the United States has chosen to give religion free play in society. The American Constitution denies to itself all competence in the area, accepting the traditional distinction between church and state as one of the principles of limited government. The immediate result has been freedom and stability for church bodies as a matter of law. But the more far-reaching effect has been that between these church bodies and government there has developed over many generations a relationship so benign that Americans as a people have never hesitated to find the hand of God operative in the affairs of state.

In Chapter 1, I try to situate this native tendency into the larger social and global challenges that confront the nation today. Few persons would be so uncritical of our country as to claim that the energies which initially formed our republic and subsequently expanded it were unambiguously religious. Precisely because Americans have tended traditionally to identify national purpose with divine purpose, there has always been a large measure of presumption and pride, as well as a certain idolatrous naiveté, mixed into popular patriotism. This must be honestly faced and dealt with as we move into our third century, or we shall lose all credibility on the international level. A new world community, which is daily becoming more conscious of it-self and more demanding of its leader-nations, is asking us questions to which we have had up to now very few satisfying answers. In Chapter 2, I try to grapple with what I believe to be the common bond between us and this new world family, namely, that dynamism for the new symbolized in our ideal of the pursuit of happiness. Because of this pursuit we have always believed that justice in the social and economic spheres must be com-patible with political and cultural freedom (which the Founders referred to as "public happiness"). What we do not recognize, even today, is that most peoples on earth are now beginning to suspect that this may be too utopian an ideal for the global village. Many would opt immediately for economic equality at the cost of free-dom, because they want to ensure a much fairer distri-bution of wealth than now seems possible under what is perceived as nothing but a mere formality of rights and duties.[2]

What is to be our future responsibility to such a world? Its peoples ask us to justify that commitment to freedom which seems to make us insensitive to the immediate global need for a fairer distribution of wealth. Will we be able to offer such justification, mak-ing cultural and political freedom as attractive to them today as it was to us in 1776? Or will the trend toward totalitarianism grow, because our dominant economic and military power continues to make nations feel, not freer in their political choices, but more dependent upon our condescension and largesse? In the first two chapters I try to understand how our religious roots and revolutionary ideals can help us come to terms with this type of question. As a nation we do not choose our values as we do merchandise in a store; they are not objects outside us but indicators of who we are and how we view reality. We therefore choose them by affirming what is deepest in ourselves, namely, our understandings of what it means to be human in civil society, what it means to be related in our public lives to both God and our neighbor, with grace and good conscience. We reach such understandings neither by overemphasizing human weakness nor by exaggerating human virtue, but simply by being ourselves, thereby responding to the ever urgent voice of religion calling individual as well as nation to self-knowledge and self-transcendence.

The second two chapters focus upon two classic social structures, law and the institutional church, which have traditionally mediated any nation's understanding of itself and its value system. The prism through which I examine these structures is the First Amendment to the United States Constitution, because it is this Amendment which has enabled freedom under law and freedom under God to be at the same time limited yet staunchly affirmed. Its guarantee of freedom of expression I find to be an extraordinary act of faith in what it means to be human in civil society, yet something which large segments of humanity still regard as a nonvalue. There is thus a strong analogy here with the act of faith made by a religious person: in each commitment there is an obscure search for an ideal which, while always going beyond one's reasons for embracing it, ever demands greater clarity and possession. Perhaps more than any other part of the Constitution, this guarantee shows that we believe that the primary purpose of our legal order is to facilitate the mutual understanding of ourselves and our quest for the commonweal. We accept whatever tension and conflict accompany such efforts because we have confidence that our judicial process will mediate our understanding and search. This is why we bestow an almost religious aura on our judiciary, especially the Supreme

Court, and why we are so shocked when we find judges without a sense of mission, who conceive of their task as merely a mechanical application of precedents.

The religion clauses of the First Amendment, examined in Chapter 4, represent a very different kind of faith commitment but with implications that are no less political and judicial. The question of what to do with churches vis-à-vis government was fundamental for the Founders, and their decision to experiment with pluralism and freedom was one with which church theology at the time could barely cope. Hence by opting for consistency with the larger American experiment in limited government, the Founders created the problem which churches have had to grapple with ever since. How is freedom under God, which is now their right, to be reconciled with a witnessing to justice under God? Government presupposes a desire for justice, and when it is absent, government as such has no resources to create it. Yet for a church to invoke its spiritual and moral authority in behalf of the rights of some against others is to claim for itself as an institution an influence upon society which many would question. The issue here is whether the freedom guaranteed the churches should enable them to be more concerned with society's problems or more concerned with their own. Ought they give voice to how a citizen's freedom is to be used virtuously, or is this the prerogative of the citizen alone? If they render judgment on some moral imperative in the political order, are they usurping the state's right or supporting it? The final chapter gives no definitive answers to these questions, but asks that they be looked at honestly by the government as well as by the churches, and especially by the individual citizen who pledges allegiance to both.

1

A NEW ORDER
FOR THE AGES

The Republic
as an Almost Chosen People

The common theme of this book may be seen at a glance on the reverse side of a United States one-dollar bill. In the center is the national motto, "In God We Trust," solemnly chosen as such by the Congress of the United States during the presidency of Dwight D. Eisenhower. To the left and right are the two sides of the Great Seal of the United States chosen by the same Congress two centuries earlier. On one side of the Great Seal there is an unfinished pyramid, symbol of the unfinished republic and its strength, above which there is an eye inside a triangle surrounded by rays of light, symbol of that divine favor in which the young nation placed its hope and confidence. This is made explicit in the Latin words just above the eye, adapted from Virgil's *Aeneid: annuit coeptis,* "He has favored our undertaking." At the base of the pyramid are engraved Roman numerals for the year 1776, below which are emblazoned the words that announce the Founders' belief in what they had actually done through God's favor: *novus ordo seclorum,* "a new order for the ages." The original of this phrase is the guiding line of Virgil's Fourth Eclogue, a nativity hymn celebrating the world's salvation in the phenomenon of birth. Seeing the human species regenerating itself constantly and forever, Virgil had written: "The great order of the ages is born anew." But the Founders believed that what they had done was not a "great" order of ages repeating itself, but a "new" order of ages, and hence the change in wording. The year 1776 marked for them the start of something different, an entirely new story never told before, an absolutely new beginning.

So strong was this sense of new beginning that Benjamin Franklin, Thomas Jefferson, and John Adams originally proposed that it be symbolized on the Great Seal by Moses crossing the Red Sea. The exodus of Israel from Egypt was for them a symbol of liberation and future freedom, as well as the conquest of a promised land. "The basic reality in their life was the analogy with the children of Israel," says Daniel Boorstin, writing of revolutionary times. "They conceived that by going out into the wilderness they were reliving the story of the Exodus."[1] The American Revolution was thus not only the foundation of a new body politic but the beginning of a specific national history, "the first new nation," the first major colony successfully to break away through revolution from that colonial rule which was at the time everywhere taken for granted.[2] "I always consider the settlement of America," wrote John Adams in 1765, "as the opening of a grand scheme and design in Providence for the illumination of the ignorant and the emancipation of the slavish part of mankind all over the earth."[3]

This sense of destiny is certainly not peculiar to Americans; it is an ingredient in the self-consciousness of every people who try to define their corporate sense of direction through history. What is peculiar to Americans is the interpretation given by the Founders to this formative experience: they translated it into the experience of Israel's exodus from Egypt. In other words,

Americans were not just a rebellious people; they were a chosen people, whose subsequent history was to be built upon a faith experience. This historical faith experience is, I believe, a phenomenon of major significance to the nation. People have given it various names in recent years: "the religion of the republic," "societal religion," "civil religion," "democratic faith." In this first chapter I would like to address myself to this phenomenon and to divide my treatment into three parts: first, the phenomenon in some of its historical manifestations; second, the legitimacy of speaking of it as a "religion"; third, its power to influence people in America today.

I

We should note at the outset that there is a very fundamental theological question involved in seeking to talk about the "religious" dimension of a national experience, namely, the extent to which God manifests himself in and through the institutions of human culture. We should expect that the Christian tradition, following out the full implications of the incarnation, would strongly affirm this. The tradition has indeed done so, but with caution and reserve, because such affirmation always involves a twofold danger. On the one hand, there is the perennial tendency to identify God with those cultural enterprises through which he reveals himself, thereby losing all sense of his transcendence and judgment; on the other hand, there is the opposite tendency so to emphasize God's transcendence that the world of public experience gradually gets pushed outside the ambit of his self-communication. We may state the problem even more pointedly in terms of grace: one extreme tends to ignore the ambiguity of public structures and their need of transforming grace; the other extreme hardly recognizes the social dimension of grace at all, preferring to emphasize instead God's self-gift to the individual, his direct influence upon the human heart.

A middle ground can be found between these two extremes only if we remember that revelation and grace are two aspects of the single reality of God's self-manifestation, the correlative of which is the sinfulness of all things human. Hence to affirm that God reveals himself through public processes is to affirm also that such processes are projections not only of human creativity but also, and necessarily, of the human propensity to do evil. These two correlatives of divine initiative and human frailty must be constantly kept in mind as we look for the sacral dimension in that public experience which is the American dream. I believe we can affirm that this experience has been and continues to be a bearer of God's self-revelation and grace. But in order to do so we must be ready to acknowledge our nation to be a vehicle for evil as well as for good. We must be willing to apply Paul's words to our public as well as to our private experience: "Where sin increased, grace abounded all the more."[4]

Having noted this underlying theological question, we are in a better position to keep in perspective the historical experience which Americans have had of themselves as a people under God. Let us begin with the observations of two visitors from other lands, the first from France in the early nineteenth century, the second from England in the mid-twentieth. Alexis de Tocqueville wrote a massive study of American life, in which he said in 1835 that "there is no country in the world where the Christian religion retains a greater influence over the souls of men than in America."[5] Gilbert K. Chesterton believed the same in 1922: America, he wrote, is "a nation with the soul of a church, . . . the only nation in the world that is founded on a creed. That creed is set forth with dogmatic and even theological lucidity in the Declaration of Independence."[6] If Chesterton had looked to the author of this Declaration, Thomas Jefferson, he would have found a prime example of this American religious sense: Jefferson, in his Second Inaugural Address as President, spoke of "that Being in whose hands we are, who led our forefathers as Israel of old, from their native land and planted them in a country flowing with all the necessaries and comforts of life, who has covered our infancy with His providence and our ripe years with His wisdom and power."[7] Just a few years earlier George Washington had spoken in the same way in his First Inaugural Address: "No People can be bound to acknowledge and adore the invisible hand, which conducts the affairs of men, more than the People of the United States. Every step, by which they have advanced to the character of an independent nation, seems to have been distinguished by some token of providential agency."[8] Shortly thereafter Washington proclaimed the celebration of Thanksgiving Day in November, as an occasion for public prayer to acknowledge this care and protection of God. Max Lerner has concluded quite correctly from such instances that historically Americans have tended to find their religious faith in various forms of belief about their own existence as a people.[9]

The experience of Israel, then, is what provided the earliest symbolism and chief inspiration for America's national faith. But while this Biblical event of covenant is the archetype of God's presence to America, the immediate vehicle of his revelation was always seen to be events in the national experience itself. The Revolution, for example, was transformed into the final act of exodus, and the documents it produced, the Declaration of Independence and the Constitution, took on the

aura of sacred scriptures. Reverence for these documents has survived the most minute scrutiny as well as
some severe criticism over the years, especially of those
truths which the Founders perceived as self-evident.
The source of this reverence is without doubt an intense communal remembrance of the events that gave
these documents birth, a remembrance that has in turn
shielded both events and documents from the onslaught of time and circumstance.[10]

Such remembrance has been operative in a very different way, however, in regard to that other pivotal
event of American history, the Civil War. The self-
understanding achieved through this great national ag-
ony was traumatic. Robert Bellah describes at some
length how the war added a whole new symbolism to
the public consciousness, relating to death, sacrifice,
and rebirth, a symbolism that found a voice of extraordinary power in Abraham Lincoln, because he himself
embodied it in his life as well as in his martyr's death.
Lincoln's interpretation of the war focused upon it both
as a time of testing for the Union and as a time of God's
judgment upon an unfaithful people. His Gettysburg
Address and Second Inaugural Address sounded together the note of judgment and expiation, and immediately took their place alongside the Constitution
and Declaration of Independence. "If we shall sup-
pose," he said as he took his oath of office for the second
time, "that American slavery is one of those offenses
which, in the providence of God, must needs come, but
which, having continued through His appointed time,
He now wills to remove, and that He gives to both
North and South this terrible war as the woe due to
those by whom the offense came, shall we discern
therein any departure from those divine attributes
which believers in a living God always ascribe to Him?
. . . If God wills that . . . [this war] continue until all

wealth piled by the bondsman's two hundred and fifty years of unrequited toil shall be sunk, . . . it must be said 'the judgments of the Lord are true and righteous altogether.'" This was an echo of Gettysburg, where Lincoln had insisted that from all the blood and suffering there had to come "a new birth of freedom."[11]

The American psyche was shaken by the Civil War as by no other event, unless perhaps by that congeries of events in the 1960's, on which we shall comment later. The Civil War brought recognition that this land of freedom and equality was also a land of oppression, that its people had responded to the call of God in a profoundly ambiguous way, that at the heart of the American dream there was betrayal. In the Dred Scott decision of 1857 the Supreme Court made this betrayal explicit for millions of black Americans. Blacks were not covered by the Constitution, said Chief Justice Roger B. Taney; they were never intended to share the "rights and privileges, and rank, in the new political body throughout the Union."[12] Eventually America had to face up to this falsifying of its noblest ideals. It had to admit to concealment of its inadequacies as "land of the free." The "new order for the ages" turned out to be not so new after all: the old oppressions were still there. As the nation stood before God it had to acknowledge that it was, in Lincoln's telling phrase, "his almost chosen people."[13]

Memorial Day was instituted shortly after the Civil War to give ritualistic expression to the reality behind Lincoln's images of death and rebirth. Its observance is still a major event in the towns and smaller cities of America, as is Thanksgiving Day in the life of the nation as a whole. Memorial Day was an acknowledgment that just as the people had been one in their complicity with slavery so now they would be one in their halting efforts to bring liberty and happiness equally to all Americans.

Yet for another century these efforts would be just that: halting. The sad legacy of the Reconstruction period revealed the fact that the country did not really act as though slavery had contradicted the American dream. In 1883, for example, the Supreme Court took the teeth out of the Civil Rights Act of 1866. Soon afterward it diverted the Fourteenth Amendment to the protection of business, and eventually it legitimized segregated public schools. Indians, women, and the poor were all objects of the same unconcern. It is embarrassing now to remember that this period in our history was one of economic exploitation, militant Anglo-Saxonism, and outright military imperialism.[14] The symbols of the national ideal continued to be reverenced and preserved, but somehow in the daily lives of people they were not working.

II

What I have been talking about up to now has been described as "the realm of motivational myths."[15] A myth, in this sense, is that which declares man's relationship to the world of reality; it preserves a concrete human experience not by describing it so much as by transforming it, by giving insight into its meaning, so that it provides moral and spiritual motivation for individuals and society. As an empirical fact, the origin of the United States was the successful rebellion of thirteen colonies against England. But this event was immediately perceived in terms of a special destiny under God, an "exodus" to a future in which America was chosen to demonstrate for all the world the possibilities for freedom and happiness in a constitutional republic. This was the "new order for the ages," and it imposed upon Americans the duty to see to it "that government of the people, by the people, for the people, shall not

perish from the earth." Failure in this duty was at root
an infidelity to God and hence stood under his judgment. The purposes of God for America might not at
any given time be seen clearly, but the conviction was
always there that God indeed had a purpose, and that
it would eventually be revealed experimentally in the
unfolding events of history. This conviction constituted
the faith of America, its myth, its set of shared convictions, the symbolic illumination of meaning behind its
civil and political society.

The question to be asked at this point, then, is, What
value judgment are we to place upon this motivational
myth? Its motivating force has not always been for the
good in American life. Our judgment must take full
measure of the ambiguity contained in the symbol. Ernest Lee Tuveson, for example, has documented in
frightening detail the consequences of our so-called
"manifest destiny," by which we have over the years
forced other peoples into thinking as we do through
economic pressure or brute force. The platitude about
saving the world for democracy he exposes for the racist slogan that it was, justifying Anglo-Saxon superiority
and the messianic illusion that we were saviors of the
world. Albert J. Beveridge expressed this arrogant self-
righteousness in capsule form at the turn of the century
when he said on the floor of the United States Senate:
"God has not been preparing the English-speaking and
Teutonic peoples for a thousand years for nothing but
vain and idle self-contemplation and self-admiration.
No. He made us master organizers of the world to establish system where chaos reigned. . . . And of all our
race He has marked the American people as His chosen
nation to finally lead in the redemption of the world."[16]

Mark Twain once remarked that religion is pretty
dangerous stuff if you get it wrong. In recent years two
strongly negative judgments have been made on the

American myth, both insisting that it has gotten its
religion all wrong. One judgment says that the myth is
idolatry, the other that it is a totally secularized piety.
Let us briefly examine each of these before dealing
with a third and more benign judgment, which I would
tend cautiously to favor.

The accusation of idolatry has been made in no un-
certain terms by Will Herberg. In his influential study
from the 1950's, *Protestant—Catholic—Jew,* Herberg
characterized the phenomenon we are discussing as
"the American way of life," the sanctification of ideas,
values, and beliefs common to Americans as Americans.
The Judeo-Christian faith, he said, has always judged
such a religion to be incurably idolatrous. "The burden
of this criticism," he continued, "is that contemporary
religion is so naively, so innocently *man-centered.* Not
God, but man—man in his individual and corporate
being—is the beginning and end of the spiritual system
of much present-day American religiosity. . . . God is
conceived as man's 'omnipotent servant,' faith as a
surefire device to get what we want."[17] The result, he
feels, has been a direct exploitation of religion for economic and political ends, its use as a spiritual reinforce-
ment of national self-righteousness and a spiritual au-
thentication of national self-will. Recently Charles P.
Henderson, Jr., wrote a study entitled *The Nixon Theology,* in which he argues from the writings of the former
President that his religion is a form of national self-
worship without any element of higher judgment. In
Henderson's analysis Richard Nixon's first and second
inaugural addresses appear as sustained hymns to
American innocence: "I know America. I know the
heart of America is good." Henderson concludes that
Mr. Nixon "systematically appropriates the vocabulary
of the church—faith, trust, hope, spirit—and applies
these words not to a transcendent God but to his own

nation."[18] Whether Henderson's judgment is correct or not, we must surely admit that Mr. Nixon consistently said what millions of Americans wanted to hear.

A second accusation has been made that the phenomenon we are dealing with is far too amorphous to be dignified with the name of idolatry. It is much better described as "religion in general," the least common denominator of the three religious faiths professed by the majority of Americans. Some have urged that the phrase not be understood pejoratively, since young people today are in fact attracted and enriched by this common denominator, while they tend to shy away from individual church membership associated with the adult "establishment." Yet the phrase has mostly had a pejorative connotation. Such "religion," it is said, is an intellectual abstraction, a distillation of what churches and synagogues profess, engendering none of the intense loyalty and commitment which Americans have historically given to concrete doctrines and institutions. According to this view what we have here is a secularization of traditional piety, an instrument used by politicians and businessmen to achieve national goals by pouring religious balm upon such things as the American work ethic and its pragmatism. There is a God, yes, and the Bible speaks about him, but the only conclusions we may draw from this are those long since drawn by Norman Vincent Peale and the Reverend Ike: if God is really the decent fellow he is supposed to be, then of course he must favor America and smile innocuously on all our undertakings. Americans can therefore continue to missionize the world, uncritical of themselves and their values, and above all unafraid of any divine reckoning.[19]

A third judgment on the American myth admits that the first two judgments are correct up to a point. That point is where the worst in the practice of a given tradition separates itself from the best of its beliefs. What some call "American religion" and others "civil religion" *does* involve idolatry and crass utilitarianism, but these worst elements should not be identified with the whole. "Contrary to Will Herberg's much popularized misunderstanding," writes historian Sidney Mead, American religion "is *not* 'the American way of life,' any more than the Christian faith *is* the way of life that ordinary professing Christians commonly exemplify in their everyday activities." In other words, critics take as typical the worst in the tradition of civil religion, conveniently overlooking the fact that spokesmen like Lincoln, who belonged to no church, consistently drew upon belief in a transcendent God in order to censure America.[20] The common religious understanding which America has had of itself has thus sometimes been praiseworthy and sometimes not. The fact is that we have used religion simply as a means to further national goals, and whenever this has happened there has always been perversion, no matter how noble the ends. This is not to say that there should be no relation at all between the religious commitment of Americans and their country's goals; such a relation has always existed. The issue here is rather what should be the proper relationship.

This proper relationship, Robert Bellah suggests, is one in which national purposes are the handmaiden of the fundamental value commitments that have historically given our nation meaning. These commitments appear in the religious symbols and rituals growing out of the American experience interpreted in the dimension of transcendence. In other words, while there has always been a belief that God is active in our history, there has also existed the conviction that if he is not to cease to be God, his designs cannot simply be identified with the designs of the country at any given time. This

constant awareness is the one central strand in American civil religion which does not make the nation ultimate. Such an awareness is in clear continuity with the
Judeo-Christian tradition, out of which it is, at least in
part, an organic development.[21] Hence there is a sense
in which America can function as the "church" that
Chesterton sensed it to be, namely, as an institution
whose ideals and goals bind a people together under a
sovereign God and give them a genuine apprehension
of his transcendent reality. Understood in this way, the
"religion of the Republic is essentially prophetic, which
is to say that its ideals and aspirations stand in constant
judgment over the passing shenanigans of the people,
reminding them of the standards by which their current practices and those of the nation are ever being
judged and found wanting. . . . To be committed to that
religion is therefore not to be committed to this world
as it is, but to a world as yet above and beyond it to
which this world ought to be conformed."[22]

I would tend to agree with this third judgment. It is
more congruent with the Biblical affirmation that,
while God's providence and grace are operative in all
things human, the human is nonetheless open to perversion, radical ambiguity, misinterpretation, and neglect. Yet my agreement also involves some doubts.
These do not touch the self-manifestation of God in
human affairs; in this I firmly believe. Nor do they touch
the assertion that the religion of the republic has func-
tioned historically as a true religion, giving our people
a genuine apprehension of transcendence and the
revelatory character of events. My doubts focus rather
upon the lives and aspirations of Americans today. I
think we have to ask, not whether there has been a
national faith and whether it has been good, but
whether it is still in existence; whether our traditional
symbols any longer influence public policy; whether

the American dream is still alive; whether we still hope, or feel we have any right to hope, for our republic to stand as "a new order for the ages." It is to such questions that I now wish to direct our attention.

III

I think we would agree that it is not an unmixed blessing for a people to find in their nation the symbols of ultimate meaning. This has been the case, however, for a large segment of the American population. The obvious danger is the one we already discussed: idolatry. But in the last decade the opposite danger has become much more acute, namely, a widespread disillusionment and cynicism that inevitably results whenever symbols, especially sacred symbols, become ambiguous, decay, or simply die. I, for one, would be hard put to find to any extent today the old conviction that America has been set apart by Providence; that we are bearers of transcendent norms, of eternal values, of a sacred truth. Even law-and-order people no longer seem to believe this, since their flag-waving is usually just a weapon to silence critics or to enhance the *status quo*. So muted and tentative is American faith in our time that, according to opinion polls carefully taken in 1971, 47 percent of our adult population feared that the country was headed for a breakdown. Three years after My Lai and two years before the trauma of Watergate, these same opinion polls found that the average American believed that the country's situation was worse than five years before and would be still worse five years later. Drawing upon such data in his prizewinning study, *A Religious History of the American People,* Sydney Ahlstrom reaches the following conclusion: "The decade of the sixties was a time . . . when the old foundations of national confidence, patriotic idealism, moral traditionalism and even of historic Judaeo-Christian theism, were awash. . . . The nation was experiencing a *crise de conscience* of unprecedented depth. The decade thus seemed to beg remembrance for having performed a great tutelary role in the education of America, for having committed a kind of maturing violence upon the innocence of a whole people."²³

This violence erupted suddenly during the '60s, not only in racial tensions, student protest, and the assassination of public figures but also in the visible deterioration of cities, the dislocation of moral values, and the heedless pollution of a once healthy environment. We became a society torn by riots, divided by generations, ravaged by drugs, and alarmed at the mere sight of a darkened street at night. At the same time we became aware of a more refined violence done to the poor and the old, to land laid waste for profit, and most of all, perhaps, to women, who at long last began to voice indignation at the denial of their rights as public and private persons. Yet all the while, as one astute observer has noted, we were able somehow to connive with such violence by preoccupying ourselves as a people with skin care, clothes care, lawn care, floor care, appliance care, car care, and pet care. The disclosure and recognition of all this now brings shame and remorse to many, and to many others self-hatred and despair. They see the emblems of their once beloved country disfigured, while the traditional symbols of loyalty and national reverence lie impotent beneath a weight of frustrated hope and withdrawn affection.

In *Nashville,* Robert Altman tries to capture on the screen some of the pain and irony in this shattering of the American dream. "We must be doing something right to last two hundred years," sings a performer at the start, and then we are overwhelmed with a two-and-a-half-hour cascade of vulgarity, deceit, greed, cruelty, and hysteria. At the end Altman seems to be saying that all this is the total negative of which the total positive is our extraordinary capacity for life. We are, in other words, victims of our own vitality. Our psychic anarchy is a result of our having allowed this vitality to become unrestrained, wanton, and perverse.

"Can you give me some help in my effort to be *proud* of my country again?" This question was asked not long ago by a clergyman in Philadelphia when he heard that two seminary professors were writing about America.[24] I think that this is a felt need which is growing. I know I feel it. But I also think we shall have to wait some years before this need is satisfied. We have no right to be proud today, at least if this means rejoicing in the present state of the republic. Almost twenty years ago Max Lerner observed that "America has never had to meet the great test of apparently irretrievable failure. Except for the Civil War, its history has been without sharp breaks. . . . Thus America as a civilization has been far removed from the great type-enactment of the Christian story, or the disasters of Jewish history or of the Asiatic empires: it has not suffered, died, been reborn. The weight it bears as it faces its destiny is the weight not of history but of institutions. Its great tests are still to come." Lerner was confident then that the nation would not meet these tests badly, but he added nonetheless that "it would be tragic if it had to taste disaster in order to learn the lessons of lost civilizations."[25] Obviously no one can say for certain whether disaster actually threatens us today, but who would deny that we are in a learning situation? Such learning can be painful, however, and it could well be that sometime in our future Little Rock, Kent State, Attica, and Watergate will be remembered for the same reasons as Gettysburg and Valley Forge.

This is undoubtedly the reason that so many commentators believe that the central problem for America today is how to develop some national and corporate sense of responsibility. "We cannot blame the oil producers for the irresponsible and rapacious extravagance of our vaunted 'way of life,' " said William Fulbright, speaking at Fulton, Missouri, where Winston Churchill gave his Iron Curtain speech. An even greater threat than this heedless waste of wealth, requiring much more attention, is our irresponsible use of power. Nine years earlier Fulbright had called his book on America *The Arrogance of Power,* by which he meant the tendency instinctively to rely upon force instead of intelligence. This is clearly to invite disaster, he said, yet "it is one of the perversities of human nature that people have a far greater capacity for enduring disasters than for preventing them, even when the danger is plain and imminent."[26] We Americans have too much wealth and too much power; there is too much abuse of both and too little control of either. This is what Peter Davis was trying to say in *Hearts and Minds,* his blunt and harrowing documentary on the Vietnam war. At the start of the film we hear Clark Clifford recalling the extraordinary economic, military, and industrial power which the United States found itself with at the end of the Second World War. Then for over an hour the camera shows us the nearly suicidal effects of that power when it was explained, justified, and wielded as something which we believed to be our due. American achievements are not downgraded in Davis' film; the point he is making with image after image is rather that our lack of modesty and perspective in those achievements has been fatal.

If the battered and bruised symbols of our civil religion are barely alive today, then the first reason is that as a nation we have forgotten that power means responsibility and that responsibility means that we must humbly acknowledge that the risk of evil is inextricably involved in any human exercise of power. "The American people are experiencing the dislocation that any religious group would experience when it is disclosed that their religion itself shares actively in evil. The bearer of transcendence and ultimacy is itself caught up in evil—this is a shaking experience that human beings can scarcely absorb without devastating consequences."[27] Little wonder that we have had a counterculture exemplifying all those inadequacies in the American dream which the people as a whole have tried to conceal.

The prime example of such concealment in domestic life is, of course, the way white Americans have systematically excluded black Americans from the mainstream of our cultural and economic life. Such concealment is becoming more difficult, however, because the black community has finally forced into the open the question of national responsibility for such exclusion. The disclosure of our guilt here has been painful and humiliating and constitutes the second reason for our disillusionment with the American dream. For everyone knows that our civil religion has had ample resources all along to deal with white brutality and aggression against blacks. As a nation we have a doctrine of human rights unequaled in the world for its breadth and nobility, and during the Civil War this doctrine forced the abolition of slavery. But the doctrine could not go the whole way, because the revelatory events of our national faith which inspired it were drawn almost exclusively from the history of white America. This explains our shame and frustration today: our civil religion is seen to be one of the chief creators of the dilemma which we are now calling upon it to solve. The originators and preservers of our American dream never really accepted a genuine cultural pluralism. Nor is it at all clear that we are about to do so today. At best it is problematic that we shall exercise full responsibility in this area. We may very well continue to condemn one group of Americans to an inferior status and to dismiss as utopian the ideal of a society that truly includes all its members.[28] After all, the propensity to identify one's own group as good and to project evil on outsiders is a general human problem, is it not? Must not other nations face this problem too? The answer is, Yes, they must. But in their case the future character and psyche of the country do not depend upon the answer.

This brings me now to the third and much more fundamental reason that the religion of the republic is in trouble today. The first two reasons were moral; the third is theological and concerns the interpretation of the central symbol of our national faith: God. Historically, as we have seen, the danger has been the trivialization of God, whom we so often conceived as a deity without wrath, smiling benignly on America and casting a Nelsonian eye upon all our shortcomings. Yet even such a God was always acknowledged to be a God of power, from whom the nation had received its mission, who watched over its future, and who, if we were faithful, would crown that future with success. As a result, divine transcendence was never wholly lost by the main-line American tradition; our sense of mission and destiny, and consequent commitment to a future largely unknown, was precisely the mode by which God manifested himself to our national experience. In the language of contemporary theology, God *was* the power of our future. He was perceived as transcendent because somehow our future was also so perceived, and its bestowal upon us as a people was what illumined our location in history. "The primal myth of American identity is nothing if it is not a celebration of the future as the ultimate reality of our national existence. This perception . . . put us on a linear course in contrast to the prevailing cyclical national myths that dominated previous nations—and it did so long before Marxism performed the same feat for the societies of the East."[29]

The disillusionment brought by events of the last decade has thus been precisely an alienation from the future. These events encourage the belief that our country really has no future to believe in, and that efforts to create one by articulating a national purpose under God are ill-conceived and of no avail. This experience has been so devastating because the vast majority of our people still *want* to believe in the American dream; they still *want* to put faith in a God who gives us a mission and calls us to a destiny that is ours alone. They are disturbed by talk of confining American ideals to the empirical and the pragmatic, or of relegating the pursuit of the truth to the private sphere alone. Such talk seems to encourage a purposeless society, whose institutions have no content but are simply channels through which any kind of content may flow. If this were to become our nation's meaning, then which direction we were going would be unimportant; the only concern we would have is whether democratic procedures were meticulously observed along the way. Once again, it is not at all clear, at least not to me, what the final result here is going to be. Yet if our future American identity contains no reference at all to God as the power of our future, who works through the structures of society and manifests himself in public affairs, then there will surely be no room for belief in any "new order for the ages," and even to speak of an "almost chosen" people will be to mouth an irrelevancy.

IV

I do not wish to exaggerate the threefold irresponsibility I have been discussing: our abuse of power, our treatment of black Americans, and the emptying of our central religious symbol. Each new generation, I know, believes it has more problems than the last. But let us note one entirely new factor in our national life which no former generation has had to face. I mean the great issue of the place of our country in the world community that began to form itself at the end of the Second World War. Everything we now do as a nation must be played out upon a global scale. We are gradually being forced to exchange the goals of national self-interest for the goals of citizens of the world, to struggle, in John F. Kennedy's words, "against the common enemies of man: tyranny, poverty, disease and war itself." The peoples of the earth are pressing us for our identity, yet we hesitate. This hesitation is so painful to us not because other nations do not also have identity crises (we know they do), but because we are so keenly aware that upon *our* shoulders has fallen the burden for developing some kind of visible and coherent world order. Hence our frantic effort to reexamine the symbols of our original identity. In our new world role shall we continue to understand ourselves in the light of a transcendent reality? Shall we retain that eschatological hope in the future which inspired the beginning of the American dream?

Let me end this chapter, however, with a statement rather than a question. I think we have less illusion about ourselves today than we had twenty years ago; we are less inclined to define ourselves as purer than the rest of the world. If we are more irresponsible, we are also more conscious of that irresponsibility, more capable of accepting our darker side. We no longer feel compelled to idealize our Founders: we can acknowledge, for example, that, in his own way, Thomas Jefferson was a racist, that while he wrote the Declaration of Independence, holding all men to be equal, black slaves were working in his garden. This humility is a sign of hope. It can lead us to combine intense patriotism with intense criticism, to say, with William Lee Miller, "Of thee, nevertheless, I sing."[30] This humility is also a sign of faith, for we have no certainty at all that we shall continue to signify as a nation; God has promised no such thing. Commitment to any way of life involves risk: we cannot rig the future so as to know beforehand that we are betting on a sure thing. As an "almost chosen" people we may, as Lincoln said, "nobly save or meanly lose the last best hope on earth." If we do lose it, it will be because we have forgotten that the divine judgment is harshest on those who are most favored. But if we save it, then it will be because we have had faith that this American dream of destiny under God, however finite and fragile, will not in the end perish from the earth.

2

THE PURSUIT
OF HAPPINESS

Self-evident Truth
as an Energizing Force

Samuel Johnson once said that people needed to be reminded more often than they needed to be instructed, and I suggest that we Americans need to recall more than we need to celebrate. The quality of our national memory is going to condition the quality of our national project. Memory of our beginnings must inevitably challenge us to come to terms with the ideals of those who began. Shall we accept responsibility for carrying on these ideals today, founding our republic upon them anew, or shall we conceive of ourselves differently, modifying those aspirations of our past or exchanging them for totally other modes of thought? In either case we ought to know what we are doing; we ought not to separate ourselves from our memory, for a nation so separated is helpless before the onslaught of time and must eventually be diminished.

I do not suggest by this that answers to present problems are to be found in our past. Obviously they cannot; the questions we ask simply could not have been asked by the Founders, because they were living in their world, not ours. When we interrogate their world, we find nothing at all like the summons our country has received today to participate in a global enterprise, in which massive social change is about to displace much of the conceptual frameworks of East and West. What we do find in their world, however, to the extent that we scrutinize it closely, is the substantive content of our tradition as a people. This we do by applying the tradition to ourselves in our new situation, thereby disclosing not only the true meaning of the past for us now but also the true meaning of our present. The only condition is that this reappropriation of our tradition be critical, not nostalgic or sentimental, a stimulus for new self-understanding and not a palliative.[1]

If, then, we perform this task of recall, uniting ourselves once again with the spirit of the Founders, the one thing we cannot fail to recognize is that theirs was a revolutionary spirit. This means that it contained two elements: a serious concern for the stability of the new body politic and an exhilarating awareness of the human capacity for beginning. These two elements, notes Hannah Arendt, the concern with stability and the spirit of the new, became opposites in the aftermath of the Revolution, the one becoming identified with conservatism, the other with liberalism. "From which it unfortunately seems to follow that nothing threatens the very achievements of revolution more dangerously and more acutely than the spirit which has brought them about."[2] Hence the question to which I address myself in the pages that follow: Must this revolutionary spirit of the Founders remain the experience and prerogative of their generation alone? Is it to be lost to all of us, their descendants? The revolutionary world in which we live has good reason to believe so, for America today has surely become symbolic of the *status quo,* perhaps the leading counterrevolutionary force of the century, impeding abroad what it has always defended at home, namely, the right to reach political solutions by an unhampered conflict between interested parties. As a people we have become terrified at the sight of another people attempting to create a new political realm, exactly what we ourselves attempted and accomplished two hundred years ago.

My own belief is that the future of our country and the type of role it plays in the global community hinges upon whether or not it recovers this revolutionary spirit of the Founders. To explain why this is so, I would like first to focus upon the meaning behind a single potent phrase from the Declaration of Independence, "the Pursuit of Happiness," and then to evaluate the extent to which the dynamism behind this phrase is operative in America today. We shall then be able to explore more realistically the larger implications of this dynamism for the world as a whole, and to ask what America, as it enters its third century, has to contribute to the future of human life on earth.

I

I wish to preface what I have to say about the Declaration of Independence by some remarks on textual interpretation made several years ago by the French philosopher Paul Ricoeur. "The sense of a text," says Ricoeur, "is not *behind* the text, but in front of it. It is not something hidden but disclosed. What has to be understood is not the initial situation of discourse but what points toward a possible world. . . . To understand a text is to follow its movement from sense to reference; from what it says to what it talks about. . . . Therefore, it is not the initial discourse situation which has to be understood, but that which . . . points toward a world toward which bursts the reader's situation as well as that of the author. Understanding is not directed toward an author who is to be resuscitated. It does not even address his situation. It turns toward the propositions about the world opened up by the text's refer-

ences. Understanding the text is to follow its movement
from the sense to its reference, from what it says to that
about which it talks. Beyond my situation as reader,
beyond the author's situation, I offer myself to the possible modes of being-in-the-world which the text opens
up and discovers for me."³ According to Ricoeur, then,
both author and reader of a text are really looking beyond it. The text does indeed point to what already
exists, but it then discloses something not yet in existence but possible, namely, a mode of being which both
author and reader may, however obscurely, dream of
actualizing in their lives. Such disclosure can be made,
however, only to someone who truly searches for it. So
let us search for the meaning of the pursuit of happiness
in the Declaration, first, for what the text points to as
already in existence, and then, for what it discloses of
the possible in our lives.

A five-man committee of the Continental Congress
put the Declaration together between June 11 and July
4, 1776: Thomas Jefferson, John Adams, Benjamin
Franklin, Roger Sherman, and Robert Livingston. Jefferson, the principal author, said of the event almost
fifty years later: "Neither aiming at originality of principle or sentiment, nor yet copied from any particular
previous writing, it was intended to be an expression of
the American mind, and to give to that expression the
proper tone and spirit called for by the occasion."⁴
These words are both honest and revealing: they indi-
cate that the men of the Revolution were consumers
rather than producers of ideas. Indeed, the grandeur of
the Declaration consists not so much in the originality
of its thought as in the fact that it was "the perfect way
for an action to appear in words."⁵ However, these
words had to show that the action in question was
grounded in some absolute, for the simple reason that
in the minds of people at the time such an absolute gave

to their revolution its whole energizing force. Hence the majestic second sentence: "We hold these Truths to be self-evident, that all Men are created equal, that they are endowed by their Creator with certain unalienable Rights, that among these are Life, Liberty, and the Pursuit of Happiness." We have here, without any doubt at all, an expression of the highest political aspirations of humanity, a goal toward which all truly human governments must strive. And yet for all its nobility of phrase, the sentence is not without its problems. I would like briefly to discuss two: the conviction that the truths in question are self-evident, and the belief that the pursuit of happiness is an unalienable natural right which every political society must foster and protect.

Jefferson had originally written: "We hold these truths to be sacred and undeniable," apparently in order to emphasize their divine origin. It was Adams and Franklin who changed this to "self-evident,"[6] presumably because the word better underlined the absolute and transcendent nature of the truths in question, for which no argument or persuasion was necessary. But this was not because they thought that the truths they were enunciating could compel assent in the same way as the statement that two plus two make four. They recognized that some prior agreement did have to be reached. This is undoubtedly why they all preferred to begin with *"We hold* these truths to be self-evident," and not with "these truths *are* self-evident." What was this prior agreement, long since reached, from which self-evidence followed? It was, of course, the existence of God, who by his act of creation orients every human creature toward the goals of life. This common dependence of all human beings upon a Creator is what constitutes their equality, and endows them with rights freely to pursue their personal destinies in society. If such rights do indeed belong to men and women precisely as human, then it follows that they are unalienable and hence exempt from all arbitrary government action. Any arbitrary interference with them would clearly be an affront to the dignity of the human person. However, all this is self-evident only if one first believes in a God from whom we receive in creation our corporate destiny in society. In other words, the self-evidence of which the authors speak was founded upon a prior and transcendent faith experience.[7]

This becomes even clearer if we consider the phrase that has contributed so much to our specifically American ethos: the pursuit of happiness. Howard Mumford Jones begins a full-length study of the concept by calling it a "glittering generality," adding that it is "as fundamental, as baffling, as confused, and as interesting an idea as ever appeared in a state paper. It is a notion impossible to define and difficult to forget." He notes too how this concept "underlies many of our activities in religion, government, education, business, amusement, and social psychology today."[8] In the drafting of the Declaration it was Jefferson who made the initial decision to place the pursuit of happiness among the natural rights of man, to be furthered by government along with life and liberty. In so doing he was no rhetorical innovator, for at the time the idea had become a commonplace in political thinking and had a general currency in colonial culture.[9] Nevertheless, there *was* innovation here, and it consisted in the explicit substitution of this particular natural right for that other natural right which was then almost always linked in a standard formula to life and liberty, namely, property. No objection was made by anyone in the Continental Congress to this substitution, and this fact has led Clinton Rossiter and other historians to conclude that the aim of the Founders was to proclaim in the Declaration a much more positive and creative purpose for political communities than the protection of private property. This purpose involved the explicit linking of individual happiness with individual freedom. It is not the possession of happiness in society which is the natural right but its pursuit. Whether one actually obtains happiness will thus depend on the way one uses one's freedom.[10] To say that the new nation took responsibility for facilitating the pursuit of individual happiness was to say that it aimed also at fostering individual freedom.

But there was another type of happiness at stake, and therefore another type of freedom. This was commonly called, in the political literature of the time, "public happiness." Jefferson himself used the phrase in a paper for the Virginia Convention of 1774, which anticipated the Declaration of Independence by two years.[11] He meant to distinguish such a right from the right we have just dealt with, namely, the right of subjects to be protected by government in the pursuit of private individual happiness. The right to pursue public or social happiness did not involve protection *from* something but engagement *in* something, namely, in the public realm. One pursued public happiness by pursuing the public good, by activating public power, by freely orienting the processes of government toward the goals of a free society. Public happiness was therefore synonymous with constructing the public welfare, and "depends on a virtuous and unshaken attachment to a free constitution."[12] Human destiny thus had to be pursued through social and political life as well as through private endeavor, and corresponding to this public good as goal was that public happiness to be achieved in its pursuit. Hence no one could be truly happy if happiness were to be located and enjoyed exclusively in private life. Because the Founders believed liberty to be the essence of happiness, they saw an inseparable connec-

tion between its virtuous exercise and the promotion of
the public welfare.[13]

The Declaration of Independence clearly intended,
from all evidence, that happiness be understood in this
twofold sense. But it intended more: it conceived such
happiness not as something already in existence and
therefore to be found, but as something to be created.
The word "pursuit" meant for the Founders action in
the public and private spheres to create something
new, the activation of free initiative for one's own good
and that of society. This pursuit was an unalienable
right because it flowed from human freedom, in the
same way as its self-evidence followed from belief in a
Creator who, as one Founder said, "surely wills the
happiness of his Creatures," and "did not make men to
be unhappy."[14] However, even though the pursuit itself was declared to be a natural right, that which was
pursued was never thought to be natural at all, but
rather to be the product of human imagination and
ingenuity. Happiness is what an individual or society
decides it to be, which is the reason that different individuals and different societies can pursue very different goals in life. This pursuit can become for both individual and nation at any given time an extraordinary
energizing force, moving them into a future as yet only
dimly perceived. Those who carried out the American
Revolution experienced this, and as long as the memory of their action lasts, the world can never again be
as if they had not existed. What energized them was the
self-evident truth that men and women are created to
pursue, as individuals and as society, what they see to
be their private and public good. Hence what the Declaration of Independence discloses as possible for us
today, to use the categories of Paul Ricoeur with which
we began, is that we too can be energized by this same
self-evident truth, that we can still begin something

new, something which we ourselves decide. In no sense are we bound to the routine and the predictable, either in private or in public life. To the extent that we feel ourselves to be so bound, to be on some treadmill of the necessary, to that extent we have lost the revolutionary spirit; we have lost the capacity to recall and have become a people without a memory, not knowing whence they have come.

II

Let us scrutinize our American present a little more closely now. Just how far is this dynamism from our American past operative today? I doubt if anyone will dispute the fact that Americans generally have lost the awareness that their republic began with a revolution. The urge for stability, so much part of the original revolutionary experience, has virtually blotted out that other essential element, the drive to give birth to the new. As we noted already, these two elements, conservation and revolution, now tend to be thought of as opposites. Not long ago a group of students in Indianapolis showed copies of the Declaration of Independence to several hundred people and asked them to sign it. Most refused; some thought it sounded rather dangerous.[15] In July of 1975, the People's Bicentennial Commission handed out copies of the Declaration in downtown Denver, without identifying it. Only one in five persons even recognized it, and one man said: "There's so much of this revolutionary stuff going on now. I can't stand it."[16] Obviously we cannot generalize from two isolated instances, but they do illustrate in their own way that half-serious definition of conservatism as the worship of dead revolutionaries. The dreams of an earlier generation of Americans were obviously quite different, and Alexis de Tocqueville wrote of them with admiration in 1835: "In that land the great experiment of the attempt to construct society upon a new basis was to be made by civilized man; and it was there, for the first time, that theories hitherto unknown, or deemed impracticable, were to exhibit a spectacle for which the world had not been prepared by the history of the past."[17]

I said at the start that our problem is one of recall, but actually it goes much deeper. The question we have to ask is, Do we have anything at all to contribute today to that original revolutionary enterprise? For it is clear that the Founders did expect each new generation to contribute, since the enterprise was originally, and continues to be, the product of human reason reflecting upon human experience at a given time in history. Surely this is what Jefferson meant when he said that each generation ought to have the power "to begin the world over again," and that it would be unfortunate indeed if we should ever be twenty years without some kind of rebellion.[18] Far from manifesting an unconcern for stability, as some have claimed, these much-quoted words seem to me to point rather to Jefferson's desire that the people always retain and activate, in their own way and at their own point in history, that second essential element of the revolutionary spirit, the drive to give birth to the new. The Founders obviously wanted to stabilize the republic, and actually did so with the Constitution. Indeed, our Revolution was successful precisely because it was so quickly "constituted," and therefore prevented from drifting toward new despotism, as happened in the case of so many nineteenth- and twentieth-century revolutions. But such stability, however necessary, always remains external. It touches none of the deepest levels of the psyche and affects none of our wellsprings of hope and fear. The second element does, however, and hence it cannot be legislated for, but must be constantly renewed in the human heart. Its life is that of the spirit, with its own rhythms and its own reasons. This second element, the drive to give birth to the new, is the one we have a problem with today. Because its rhythms are at a low ebb just now, it will not be enough for us simply to perform our task of recall. We must also face up to the challenge it brings to internalize and to activate anew the Founders' original revolutionary experience.[19]

This challenge comes to us, I think, from two sources. The first is the phenomenon of America as a business civilization dominated by technology. We began in the last century to produce articles for use; with greater prosperity we aimed at luxury and beauty; we now aim much of our production at obsolescence. Our business culture in turn has engendered in us the idea that happiness is to be found in a high standard of living and that *this* is the primary goal to be pursued by society. The consequent temptation is to equate the freedom of the republic with free enterprise, to think that wealth and economic well-being are the *results* of our freedom. Whereas the Founders' experience was just the opposite. The abundance of natural wealth in colonial America is what enabled them to concentrate upon the pursuit of something beyond mere well-being. They did not seek their independence either to escape from poverty or to increase productivity.[20] The happiness they sought was to be found not in consumption but in creation. Material possessions, bodily sufficiency, were the means to facilitate this new creative experience. To reduce the dynamism of self-evident truth in the Declaration of Independence to freedom to produce and to consume would have appeared to them the height of banality. This banality would have been even more startling if they had heard it uttered in a world where everyone has come to depend upon everyone else, yet where some peoples have nothing to consume and so cannot create at all. In such a world, if the pursuit of happiness is not a communal experience for which everyone takes responsibility, then it simply becomes a synonym for egocentricity. This was the warning of Henry Kissinger at the World Food Conference in Rome in 1974: "The current trend is obvious and the remedy is within our power. If we do not act boldly, disaster will result from a failure of will: moral culpability will be inherent in our foreknowledge."[21]

Our task of recall, then, challenges us first to ask whether our wealth has restricted our pursuit of happiness instead of expanding it, and more precisely whether it tends to isolate us from those millions of our fellow human beings around the globe now engaged in the same pursuit. As a people we have not yet answered this question, and hence arises our second and much more fundamental challenge: How do we conceive ourselves as a nation arriving at such an answer? I say that this is the more fundamental challenge because it highlights the contrast between what we and the Founders might conceive to be the nature of the democratic process. We have already seen that their assertion of self-evident truth followed from the conviction that each person was created by God. Such creation made all persons equal, not in talents or ability, but in the possession of certain unalienable rights. The pursuit of happiness was one of these rights because creation by God also meant destiny under God, a dynamic and creative movement toward what individual and society, at any given time, freely decide that happiness to be. Such free decision could be made, however, only after the democratic process had reached its term. Commitment to this process did not mean that the Founders believed that one opinion was as good as another or that right decision was a matter of majority vote (since the majority might clearly be wrong at any one time). What they believed was rather that truth would eventually emerge from the conflict of strongly held opinions, since the pursuit they were engaged in was a movement under the guidance of God. The will of the people, in other words, was finally the surest clue to the will of God; not in any simple or immediate sense, but in the more complex sense that human beings are best adapted as instruments to effect the divine purpose, and that therefore, as Lincoln later suggested, all of the people cannot be wrong all of the time.[22]

It is important that we acknowledge today that this understanding of the democratic process was essentially a matter of faith, not in the worth of any specific public policy, but in the movement of life under God. This movement was a pursuit, in which the nation found its security, not from what it did or possessed at some particular time, but from what it believed God would do to guide the pursuit itself. Hence the challenge for contemporary America to say where its confidence now lies, in what it possesses or in what it pursues? What is its faith experience? If possessions are its security, then it faces an inevitable failure of nerve in a world where whole peoples possess nothing. If as a nation we want only to rest in our present standard of living, then we really have nothing to pursue at all, and we had better freeze the democratic process lest it respond at some time to the Founders' revolutionary impulse to create the new. This impulse toward the new symbolizes the supremacy of experiment over tradition, and of process and plurality over order and structure. If, on the other hand, explicit rejection of the revolutionary spirit is too painful a thought for us, then let us recognize that we can countenance more subtle ways of inhibiting the democratic process. In recent years there has been an increase of what can only be called a kind of friendly fascism, whereby socially desirable objectives tend not to be received from the people but to be conceived in committee and imposed by bureaucracy. We have meekly submitted to such direction from above because it gives us greater security in the *status quo*, and dispenses us from the burden and risk of corporately imagining the reasonable and the new. We forget that technical and administrative decisions must eventually become sterile if cut off from larger purposes conceived and internalized by the nation as a whole. Technocracies deal not with self-evident truth, but with results, and without a faith experience these results eventually reduce themselves to the pragmatic and the dull.

We have, then, a serious challenge confronting us today if we recall the full implications of the Founders' revolutionary spirit and the nature of the pursuit to which it gave birth. We must ask: What is the happiness we now seek? What has it to do with the happiness of other peoples with whose destinies ours is henceforth inextricably intertwined? Shall we allow our democratic process full scope to seek imaginative public answers to these questions, or shall we restrict its task to finding purely technical solutions to moral problems, thereby assuring us security in possessions and banality in choice? In considering this challenge some Americans will undoubtedly say, with Howard Mumford Jones, that the Founders made an unfortunate blunder, that in making the pursuit of happiness an unalienable right they "were guaranteeing the American citizen the ghastly privilege of pursuing a phantom and embracing a delusion."[23] But others will not think the Founders deluded at all. With Karl Jaspers, one of the most sober of contemporary European philosophers, they will state their conviction that America has a larger destiny than to be content with its own well-

being. "Every Westerner has, in a sense, two countries," wrote Jaspers, "the country of his heart, his origin, his language, his ancestors, and one sure foundation of his political reality. Those fatherlands are many,
but this foundation is today only one: the United States
of America."[24] Jaspers wrote these words almost
twenty years ago, and it is not at all clear how many
Westerners would feel this way today. But I feel this
way. And at the risk of appearing somewhat chauvinis-
tic, I would like to explain why a recapture of our original revolutionary spirit, along with its understanding of
the pursuit of happiness, appears to me to have such
extraordinary significance for the future, not just our
future or that of the West, but the future of humankind.

III

Let me begin with the observation of another European, Gunnar Myrdal, who has looked at us with the
hard gaze of the social scientist: "America, compared to
every other country in Western civilization, large or
small, has the *most explicitly expressed* system of general ideals in reference to human interrelations. This
body of ideals is more widely understood and appreciated than similar ideals anywhere else."[25] Myrdal
is right, I think. Our country's ideals are highly valued,
and they do deal with very explicit procedures for men
and women relating to each other in society. The force
of these ideals is what was ultimately responsible for
congressional committees investigating the CIA and
the FBI. Because we valued these ideals so highly, persons of integrity were finally able to activate our moral
sensitivity to the degree needed to extricate us from
the maze of Watergate and its threat to our system of
government. The success of the civil rights movement
is another instance of our ideals allowing us to be open

and free enough to correct even long-standing contradictions to them. On the world scene we have surely not isolated ourselves from global politics; we have, on the contrary, taken part in the affairs of nations to an extent unprecedented in our history, and with the specific aim of encouraging the democratic ideal. Our free institutions, in other words, perform well whenever free men and women act responsibly.

The problem, however, is to know what is responsible action in any given situation, and this is not easy at all. It is especially difficult now because we are faced with a strange anomaly: the general acknowledgment throughout the world that America holds a key to the human future, and our response to this global expectation with hesitancy and fear that responsible commitment to the concerns of humanity may radically alter our present sense of contentment. The result of this indecisiveness has been a kind of spiritual dead point for the country, a confrontation of contradictory ideals, a paralysis of pursuit. Recently the London *Economist* commented at some length on this unsureness in our global vision. An article entitled "America's Third Century"[26] worries about what it calls "a recessional for the second great empire." I say "worries" because *The Economist* is known to be strongly pro-American. Two great empires have ruled in the first two centuries of industrial advance, says the article, the British and the American, but on the eve of our second centennial anniversary we Americans were showing the same symptoms of "a drift from dynamism" as did the British before us. World leadership is therefore liable to pass into new hands within the next generation, since extraordinary opportunities now present themselves as well as bizarre dangers, and the United States may not have the required determination to cope with either. All will depend, *The Economist* believes, on whether or not America and its leaders recognize "their manifest and now rather easy destiny of leading the rest of us toward a decent world society." This decent society must include, to be sure, material well-being, but it is well-being developed for all and shared by all, not well-being possessed by pockets of humanity and jealously guarded by the economically privileged against the economically weak.

Hence it becomes clear that this task of recall, this challenge to come to terms with our original revolutionary ideal, involves global consequences of great magnitude. Such recall may indeed induce a painful reversal of our present experience, so opposed to that of the Founders and so well characterized by *The Economist* as a "drift from dynamism." If this reversal were actually to be carried off and this dynamism from our past somehow retrieved, if we were to experience once again as a people the energizing force of pursuit, then we should immediately concern ourselves not only with the world's stability but also with its groping efforts to give birth, to create a unity and an interdependence that transcend the boundaries of nations and embrace everything earthly and human. This is what Pierre Teilhard de Chardin was referring to when he wrote in 1953: "To my mind, what is our prime concern in connection with the ultra-evolution of man is not to know how, for perhaps hundreds of thousands of years to come, we are going to feed an ever-growing population and fuel machines that are becoming ever more complicated and voracious. It will be to discover how man can maintain and increase, without check, throughout these vast periods of time, a passionate will not only to subsist but to press on: as we said, without that will every physical and chemical force we dispose of would remain heartbreakingly idle in our hands."[27]

Please understand that I am not concerned here with

governmental policy decisions, which must often be very cautious, and at times necessarily involve stability as their primary aim. My focus is not on policy, but on vision. Our leadership in the world is being questioned today not because certain of our policies are conservative, but because our vision is conservative, because we have such difficulty integrating into it the present struggle of humanity to give birth to the new. In face of a worldwide impetus for change this vision of ours is unsure, overcommitted to the *status quo,* and terribly worried that any people should conceive the revolutionary hopes that once were our own.

The economist Robert L. Heilbroner, in his *An Inquiry Into the Human Prospect,* saw this challenge of the new from a somewhat different point of view. Speaking of the developed world, especially our own nation, he said that we "face a need to identify with a special group—not one outside our borders, but beyond our reach in time—namely, the generations of the future." Where will such a concern arise? The answer, says Heilbroner, hinges upon what economists speak of as the "time discount," by which they mean the inverted telescope through which humanity looks at the future, estimating the present worth of objects to be enjoyed in the future far below the worth they would have if their enjoyment could be transferred to the present. This consequent devaluation of the future is generally considered to be an entirely "rational" response to the uncertainties of life. But, says Heilbroner, if we apply this same calculus of "reason" to the human prospect, "we face the horrendous possibility that humanity may react to the approach of environmental danger by indulging in a vast fling while it is still possible." Why indeed should we make sacrifices now to ease the lot of generations whom we will never live to see? Heilbroner believes that there is only one possible answer to this question: "It lies in our capacity to form a collective bond of identity with those future generations. . . . If mankind is to rescue life, it must first preserve the very will to live, and thereby rescue the future from the angry condemnation of the present."[28]

Both Heilbroner and Teilhard de Chardin see the same human promise and sense the same global risk: humanity is poised on the verge of a new historic era; our immediate future will be either one of the great periods of human creativity or the beginning of an extraordinary disarray. A new spirit is therefore needed among nations, a corporate recognition of interdependence, without which we shall be overwhelmed with political, social, and economic chaos. The choice we have is thus not between a whole world and a shredded-up world, but between one world and no world. This means that all hope of bourgeois tranquillity, to which America is particularly prone, must inevitably be washed out, eliminated from our horizon. A perfectly ordered society with everyone living in effortless ease, a world in a state of tranquil repose, all this has nothing to do with the tumultuous energy now seeking release all around us. Teilhard de Chardin called this energy "the zest for life" by which he meant "that spiritual disposition, at once intellectual and affective, by virtue of which life, the world and action seem to us, on the whole, luminous—interesting—appetizing." We find this energy manifested in every attempt of men and women to achieve the difficult and the new. Sir Edmund Hillary's passion for great peaks is a good example of such energy; without it there would have been no conquest of Mt. Everest. Nothing, in other words, can oblige us to move unless we want to do so. "I have often said and I repeat," wrote Teilhard de Chardin in 1951, "on mounds of wheat, coal, iron, uranium—under any sort of demographic pressure you like—the man of tomorrow will lie down and sleep if he ever loses his taste for the ultra-human. And not just any sort of taste, but a strong and deeply rooted zest; a zest constantly growing with the increase in his powers of vision and action."[29] This taste for life, this zest, is thus essentially the power of the human will to create. At one time on earth human beings could develop merely by being clothed and nourished; now they must be activated by the dynamism of free and creative choice, or their magnificent drive toward something more than well-being will grind to a miserable halt.

IV

My argument, then, is that there is an energy operative in human life whose global impact we are just coming to appreciate. All around us we see this energy's symptomatic expression: a general social disruption, spasmodic outbreaks of localized warfare, quick and disconcerting changes in the alignments of nations, new understanding of the power of racial identity. Everywhere we find unsolved crises, incomplete transitions, unplanned transformations. This is the world phenomenon par excellence which we face as we begin our third century as a nation, and I have sought in this chapter to find something in our tradition which might equip us as a people to appreciate the good in this phenomenon rather than simply to react with fear at what we see. This has led me to formulate three judgments on one essential element in that tradition, the pursuit of happiness. The first judgment focused on our past, and sought to analyze the concept as it appears in the Declaration of Independence. The Founders conceived of happiness as something to be made, not found, and held it as self-evident that every human being had the unalienable right to its pursuit. This self-evidence followed in their minds from belief in individual and corporate destiny under God, and it provided them with the energizing force to begin the new, to give reality to the creative aspirations of men and women in society.

My second judgment focused on our present, and sought some explanation for our apparent inability as a people to internalize, much less contribute to, this original revolutionary ideal. The human drive to give birth to the new now threatens us, it seems, because our business civilization has tended historically to locate happiness in consumption rather than in creation, and to make economic well-being the purpose of freedom rather than the means to facilitate the further expression of freedom in creative human endeavor. A more subtle consequence of this outlook has been a tendency to undervalue the dynamisms inherent in the democratic process itself, and to overvalue bureaucratic mechanisms ensuring stability and control.

Finally, my third judgment focused on our future, and sought to assess how high the stakes really are in America's exercise of leadership in the world today. In the face of general agreement that the species is moving toward either unity or chaos, it becomes more crucial than ever that men and women foster what Heilbroner calls the will to live and Teilhard de Chardin the zest for life. Our tradition provides us with a revolutionary ideal which can both encourage and at the same time stabilize humanity's pursuit of the new. But our task of recall must embrace the whole of this ideal, the whole of this dynamism. Otherwise we shall inhibit the global zest for life by forgetting that we too were once energized as a people by the goal of happiness and the excitement of its pursuit.

Let me draw one very brief conclusion. The Declaration of Independence electrified the world with its message of unalienable rights. Yet, as John F. Kennedy said in his inaugural address, "the same revolutionary beliefs for which our forebears fought are still at issue around the globe—the belief that the rights of man come not from the generosity of the state but from the hand of God."[30] I suggest that the real reason we undervalue the revolutionary ideal may not be economic or social or political at all, but may be rooted instead in the loss of belief that our truths are self-evident and our rights unalienable because we receive them from the hand of God. The energizing force of pursuit was much easier for Americans of a former age because their normal human fear of the adventurous and the new was counteracted by their faith in destiny under God, a conviction that their creativity was somehow a participation in God's creativity, and that human initiative from whatever quarter was therefore a challenge to be met and not a threat to be feared. No such strong conviction motivates us as a people today. Yet our responsibility for the world's future is far heavier than any carried by our forebears. Neither does history give us hope that the fire of the revolutionary spirit can ever be extinguished in the human heart. If anything, social disruption must increase as the human race continues to move into a future characterized more and more by recurring crises and global transformations. Hence we have need to perform our task of recall with special care indeed. Otherwise the American experiment with democracy under God may itself be perceived, at some later period in history, as just an early stage in a much larger movement of humanity toward a happiness ever eluding its grasp and so ever an object of pursuit.

3

FREEDOM TO SPEAK

The First Amendment
as an Anthropological Assertion

In preceding chapters I have tried to underline the religious and revolutionary character of the American dream. The analysis was mainly cultural, tracing the interrelatedness of sets of values and ideas as they appeared in our country's history and influenced our national psyche. In the present chapter, by contrast, my analysis is mainly structural. I shall deal with a particular social structure, law, and show how it acts as a vehicle through which our ideas and values live. Hence the emphasis will be on the stabilizing character of the American dream, for law is the principal institution through which a given society preserves, transmits, and revises its values. The best example of such stabilization is, of course, the Constitution of the United States, and this is why American constitutional law has become the chief interpreter of the ultimate principles of freedom upon which the nation is based.

Law as a social structure does more than stabilize, however. It is also a mirror of changing values in society. "Our Constitution is not a straitjacket," wrote Justice Louis D. Brandeis in 1922. "It is a living organism. As such it is capable of growth—of expansion and of adaptation to new conditions. Growth implies changes, political, economic, social. Growth which is significant manifests itself rather in intellectual and moral conceptions than in material things."[1] This view of Brandeis means that every interpretation of our Constitution is a development, under given conditions, of a seed planted by the Founders, a kind of political botany, aimed at preserving the essential spirit and content of the document. The ancient legal maxim, *consuetudo contra legem,* is important here: what is actually done by the people at a given time overrides the law, and the law eventually catches up.

Hence the enduring values of any given society do not present themselves ready-made. They must be continually derived from their past, enunciated and appreciated anew, and freshly applied to their contemporary setting. It is the peculiar competence of the Supreme Court to do this for the United States. Their most important function, according to Alexander M. Bickel, is to work toward "the creative establishment and renewal of a coherent body of principled rules."[2] This sorting out of the enduring values and meanings in American society takes place when the Court deals with the nitty-gritty of an actual case, so that the process is one which not only evolves a principle but immediately puts it to the test. The Justices have in this way become "teachers in a vital national seminar."[3] Their primary role is to articulate in very concrete forms America's idealized conception of itself, by which it legitimates its constraints and transforms its power into authority. "We are under a Constitution," said Chief Justice Charles E. Hughes when he was governor of New York, "but the Constitution is what the courts say it is."[4]

Nowhere has this role of the Court been more compelling in the twentieth century than in the area of the First Amendment to the Constitution: "Congress shall make no law respecting an establishment of religion, or prohibiting the free exercise thereof; or abridging the freedom of speech or of the press; or of the right of the people peaceably to assemble, and to petition the Government for a redress of grievances." There has never been any dispute among jurists that this Amendment is quite special; the dispute has come from efforts to explain this "specialness" and especially from efforts to apply it in concrete situations. "If there is any fixed star in our constitutional constellation," said the Court in 1943, "it is that no official, high or petty, can prescribe what shall be orthodox in politics, nationalism, religion, or other matters of opinion, or force citizens to confess by word or act their faith therein."[5] Just a few years earlier the Court had said that "freedom of thought and speech . . . is the matrix, the indispensable condition, of nearly every other form of freedom. With rare aberrations a pervasive recognition of that truth can be traced in our history, political and legal."[6] The First Amendment would indeed seem to be, then, an assertion of what human nature at its best should be like, a commitment to a certain mode of being human in civil society, to a particular value system which cannot be demonstrated but which in fact has never been doubted. As such, this "fixed star" is illustrative of the common American understanding of what is good and bad, providing moral and spiritual meaning for the nation's historical experience.

In what follows I limit myself to the Free Speech and Free Press Clauses of the First Amendment and explore their significance on three different levels. The first is the level of meaning and symbol, on which some unusual value judgments have been made over the years both by the Supreme Court and by legal theorists. The second level is where the most troublesome problems arise today in applying the First Amendment, namely, where speech and press inflict injury upon individuals. On this level the public exercise of First Amendment rights comes into conflict with private rights rooted outside the system of freedom of expression, thereby prompting a painful reassessment of the relationship between two very different social values. Finally, we shall examine efforts being made today to improve the system from within in order to make it function better. This is the level on which law is used, not negatively to protect the marketplace of ideas, but affirmatively to ensure equal access to it. No one denies that the system is now working badly in certain areas, especially where the mass media tend to monopolize the means of communication. But on this level too, as we shall see, there are painful reassessments when well-intentioned government intervention becomes a threat to the freedom it seeks to protect.

I

The meaning of the First Amendment guarantee has changed over the years as does the meaning of all law. "Like most revolutionaries, the Framers could not foresee the specific issues which would arise as their 'novel idea' exercised its domination over the governing activities of a rapidly developing nation in a rapidly and fundamentally changing world. In that sense the Framers did not know what they were doing." Whatever validity this guarantee has today thus derives, not primarily from its acceptance by the Founding Fathers two hundred years ago, but from its acceptance by us today. Freedom of expression, like its larger principle of self-government, is "an idea which is still transforming men's conception of what they are and how they may best be governed."[7] Throughout the nineteenth century relatively little was said about the First Amendment; it was a cherished tradition without any

specific legal constraints and with almost no occasions
calling on the courts to give it specific legal content.
Not until the present century does its career in court
decisions begin, due mainly to widespread social un-
rest. The long century of consensus ended when the
movement for industrial justice developed, because
this movement gave rise to government action aimed
both at regulating industry and at constricting freedom
of speech. At this same time there began also that long
line of judicial decisions testing the reach of the First
Amendment. In a famous dissent from a majority opinion in 1919, Justice Oliver Wendell Holmes, Jr.,
sounded what has since become a dominant theme of
these decisions. Men are naturally intolerant, he said,
but they have learned by experience that intolerance
does not pay. At least in America they have

> come to believe even more than they believe the very
> foundations of their own conduct that the ultimate good
> derived is better reached by free trade in ideas—that
> the best test of truth is the power of the thought to get
> itself accepted in the competition of the market, and
> that truth is the only ground upon which their wishes
> safely can be carried out. That at any rate is the theory
> of our Constitution. It is an experiment as all life is an
> experiment. Every year if not every day we have to
> wager our salvation upon some prophesy based upon
> imperfect knowledge.[8]

"Belief," "wager," "salvation," "prophesy," "imperfect knowledge"—this is not the language of science or
even of law, but of myth, reflecting an attitude toward
freedom of expression not unlike that of an act of faith.
"The First Amendment," said the late Judge Learned
Hand, "presupposes that right conclusions are more
likely to be gathered out of a multitude of tongues, than
through any kind of authoritative selection. To many

this is, and always will be, folly; but we have staked upon it our all."[9] This same language of belief and risk appears in what is regarded as a classic formulation of First Amendment principle. Justice Brandeis wrote it in a concurring opinion in 1927, and it will be worth quoting at length:

> Those who won our independence believed that the final end of the State was to make men free to develop their faculties. . . . They valued liberty both as an end and as a means. . . . They believed that freedom to think as you will and to speak as you think are means indispensable to the discovery and spread of political truth; that without free speech and assembly discussion would be futile; that with them, discussion affords ordinarily adequate protection against the dissemination of noxious doctrine; that the greatest menace to freedom is an inert people; that public discussion is a political duty; and that this should be a fundamental principle of the American government. They recognized the risks to which all human institutions are subject. But they knew that order cannot be secured merely through fear of punishment for its infraction; that it is hazardous to discourage thought, hope and imagination; that fear breeds repression; that repression breeds hate; that hate menaces stable government; that the path of safety lies in the opportunity to discuss freely supposed grievances and proposed remedies; and that the fitting remedy for evil counsels is good ones. Believing in the power of reason as applied through public discussion, they eschewed silence coerced by law—the argument of force in its worst form. Recognizing the occasional tyrannies of governing majorities, they amended the Constitution so that free speech and assembly should be guaranteed.[10]

In this guarantee we have, then, to quote more recent Supreme Court opinions, "a profound national commitment to the principle that debate on public issues should be uninhibited, robust, and wide-open," as well as "the assumption that the widest possible dissemination of information from diverse and antagonistic sources is essential to the welfare of the public."[11] Justice William J. Brennan, Jr., in 1972 asserted once more that "our legal system reflects a belief that truth is best illuminated by a collision of genuine advocates," and that "the genius of the First Amendment . . . is that it has always defined what the public ought to hear by permitting speakers to say what they wish."[12] These statements are all of a singular consistency, reflecting exactly the same value system which we find expressed at the time of Jefferson's First Inaugural Address. In the midst of angry and violent public debate over the Alien and Sedition Laws of 1798 he had no hesitation in saying to a troubled country: "If there be any among us who would wish to dissolve this Union or to change its republican form, let them stand undisturbed as monuments of the safety with which error of opinion may be tolerated where reason is left free to combat it." Jefferson's premise here, as he wrote in the *Bill for Establishing Religious Freedom in Virginia,* is "that truth is great and will prevail if left to herself; that she is the proper and sufficient antagonist to error, and has nothing to fear from the conflict unless by human interposition disarmed of her natural weapons, free argument and debate; errors ceasing to be dangerous when it is permitted freely to contradict them."[13]

These words of Jefferson highlight a very important implication of this American commitment to freedom of expression: each citizen must have some standards for judging what is "error of opinion" and what is not. The First Amendment obviously leaves this question of standards to the individual, but this is a far cry from counseling a total skepticism; the presumption is rather that, because it is possible to distinguish between truth and falsehood, citizens must test their thinking before they speak in order to judge for themselves whether or not it is false. Such testing will inevitably result in conflicting views of truth, and this is why the crucial factor will always be "the power of the thought to get itself accepted in the competition of the market." Alexander Meiklejohn has pointed out that these conflicting views have to be expressed, not because each is equally valid, but because each is relevant: everything worth saying ought to be said. If a view is responsibly held by anyone, it should be heard. "To be afraid of ideas, any idea, is to be unfit for self-government."[14] The problem is, of course, as many fear, that the marketplace may turn into a bullring, that ideas of racism, segregation, genocide, and fascism may eventually impose themselves by breeding attitudes and mind-sets influencing future thought and action.[15] Yet First Amendment doctrine says that unless such ideas incite to violence, coercion, or the violation of law, their expression may not be restricted. The risk here, then, is that speech which is true may indeed be unable to survive and endure speech that is false. But the alternative is to trust, not in the give-and-take of public discourse, but in what is acceptable and unacceptable to the few who for a moment hold enough power to tyrannize over the many. The first risk we have taken, the second we reject. For the American commitment is a wager, "an experiment as all life is an experiment," bringing with it ambiguity and ambivalence as well as truth. To many it is folly, "but we have staked upon it our all."

Thomas I. Emerson, in his authoritative works on the First Amendment,[16] has summarized the main premises of this American "experiment" under four headings. In maintaining a system of freedom of expression, he says, we assert that such freedom is, first of all, essential to secure individual self-fulfillment. One's mind must be free if one is to realize one's potentialities as a person. Any suppression of belief or opinion is an affront to human dignity, a placing of some under the arbitrary control of others. Secondly, freedom of expression is essential for the advancement of knowledge and the discovery of truth. No matter how certainly true or certainly false an opinion may seem to be, discussion must be kept open: the accepted opinion may turn out in the end to be erroneous and the dangerous opinion may be at least partially true and so force a rethinking of previously unchallenged thought. These first two widely held premises show that we believe this freedom to be an end in itself, a necessary element of the good society, to be measured not by whether it promotes other ends, even when these are far more inclusive, like justice and equality. These larger ends may sometimes even be hindered by such free expression, but our belief is that we ought not to seek these higher goals by suppressing the expression itself. We must rather seek them by other methods, by counter-expression, for example, or by the regulation of conduct.

The second two premises show that the freedom guaranteed by the First Amendment is not only a good in itself but also a means and a method. For this freedom is, thirdly, essential for members of a democracy to participate in decision-making at all levels of society. The successful functioning of the political process requires a wide dissemination of political ideas, whether or not they are wise or founded on truth, and self-government demands informed individual judgments. Indeed, some commentators have argued that the First Amendment guarantees only that speech which deals with matters of public interest, that is to say, with issues on which voters must cast their ballot.[17] As Emerson notes, however, such a restriction of the guarantee to purely political speech would exclude from constitutional protection vast areas of communication ranging over the fields of art, literature, science, and recreation, and as a consequence this interpretation has never gained general acceptance. Finally, freedom of expression is a method of achieving a more adaptable and stable community, of maintaining a balance between consensus and confrontation. Open discussion promotes cohesion because all have a share in decision-making. "Freedom of expression thus provides a framework in which the conflict necessary to the progress of a society can take place without destroying the society. It is an essential mechanism for maintaining the balance between stability and change."[18]

Obviously it cannot be shown that a society based on such convictions is better than one that is not. None of these premises can therefore be proven. They are part of what Emerson calls a "faith." We take a chance when we commit ourselves to the results of free expression, when we are confident that these results, however unpleasant they may be at the moment, will eventually promote the general good of society. Such a "faith" is relatively new. Peoples of past ages had very different understandings of what it means to be human. Even today such faith is denied in theory and practice by much of the world most of the time. Nor does the First Amendment point the way to unambiguous decision, but rather to compromise and accommodation. The liberty protected is thus largely a defense against encroachment, which is the indispensable condition for the attainment of any fuller freedom. In this sense the First Amendment was designed to encourage a certain degree of conflict by giving citizens the right to disagree and argue with others and with the government, to antagonize as well as to shock them. But there was confidence that, in the midst of such conflict, the nation's legal process, as interpreted by the courts, would keep the system itself in equilibrium, until such time as it was possible for some long-range consensus to emerge.

This confidence in law, however, has to be complemented in each succeeding generation by something much more subtle and complex. "Liberty lies in the hearts of men and women," said Judge Learned Hand, and "when it dies there, no constitution, no law, no court can save it; no constitution, no law, no court can even do much to help it. While it lies there it needs no constitution, no law, no court to save it."[19] Law cannot hold a nation to ideals which it is determined to betray. Law does not control people but enables them to control themselves. Its largely negative freedom, which defends self-interest, has to be supported by a more positive freedom, which fulfills this self-interest in the common good. Nor is such liberty of heart a purely technical problem, to be left for solution to bureaucrats adept at manipulation. Such manipulation destroys self-government, since it is in the nature of a republic that its members must love it to obey it. Without periodic renewal of this love of the republic neither law nor constitution will possess that inner meaning which is alone the source of their ultimate power to influence.

II

Let us move now to the second level of First Amendment understanding, the level on which freedom of speech and press come into conflict with private rights rooted outside the system of freedom of expression. "Nothing is more characteristic of the law of the First Amendment," writes Alexander Bickel, "than the Supreme Court's resourceful efforts to cushion rather than resolve clashes between the First Amendment and interests conflicting with it."[20] These efforts to cushion are a recognition by the Court that its task is not simply to adjudicate but to reconcile, and that it may not always possess the resources necessary to resolve a given conflict. Yet our entire legal system tends to be judged by the performance of this highest tribunal. In the First Amendment area the Court constantly has had to make adjustments and compromises in order to bring the functioning of American society into greater conformity with its own ideal of freedom of expression. In these decisions the members of the Court recognize their fallibility and corporate uncertainty: there are almost always dissenting opinions and the final judgment in one case is often reconsidered and modified in another, or even occasionally abandoned altogether. The Court, in other words, not only interprets an ideal, but reflects changing values of society.

These values change, of course, because people change, because new sociopolitical situations generate new ideas. Every understanding of First Amendment rights will thus inevitably bear the stamp of its social matrix. These rights may, as Justice Holmes remarked, "tend to declare themselves absolute to their logical extreme. Yet all in fact are limited by the neighborhood of principles of policy which are other than those on which the particular right is founded, and which become strong enough to hold their own when a certain point is reached."[21] Until lately it was generally assumed that there were very definite points at which First Amendment rights ended. The classic formulation of this assumption was made as late as 1942 by Justice Frank Murphy. The right of free speech, he said,

> is not absolute at all times and under all circumstances. There are certain well-defined and narrowly limited classes of speech, the prevention and punishment of

which have never been thought to raise any Constitutional problem. These include the lewd and obscene, the profane, the libelous, and the insulting or "fighting" words—those which by their very utterance inflict injury or tend to incite an immediate breach of peace. It has been well observed that such utterances are no essential part of any exposition of ideas, and are of such slight social value as a step to truth that any benefit that may be derived from them is clearly outweighed by the social interest in order and morality.[22]

This formulation reflects the clear understanding of the Court from early in the century when the question of these "points" first presented itself seriously. The year 1919 marked the beginning, with Justice Holmes saying: "The First Amendment . . . obviously was not intended to give immunity for every possible use of language. . . . We venture to believe that neither Hamilton nor Madison, nor any other competent person then or later, ever supposed that to make criminal the counseling of a murder . . . would be an unconstitutional interference with free speech."[23] There was also his famous metaphor that same year: "The most stringent protection of free speech would not protect a man in falsely shouting fire in a theatre and causing a panic."[24] In 1952, Justice Felix Frankfurter was quite explicit in regard to libel: "Libelous utterances not being within the area of constitutionally protected speech, it is unnecessary, either for us or for the State courts, to consider the issues behind the phrase 'clear and present danger.' "[25] In 1961, Justice John Marshall Harlan, referring to the Holmes quotation, gave an even more extensive list: "libel, slander, misrepresentation, obscenity, perjury, false advertising, solicitation of crime, complicity by encouragement, conspiracy. . . ."[26]

Now to lump all these areas together is to imply that they are all of a piece. It is to assert that the right in question in each carries the same weight as the constitutionally guaranteed right of free speech, and can therefore be balanced against the First Amendment and kept outside its protection. Some of these rights obviously can be so balanced. Within the last decade, however, it has become clear to the Court that others cannot. One of these is the right not to be defamed by libelous speech. The Court has weighed this right against that guaranteed by the First Amendment and has found that in certain circumstances the former must yield. The law of libel has therefore been gradually more restricted and First Amendment protection gradually more extended. The same development has taken place in the case of laws against obscenity. The Court has decided that the individual and short-term advantage of more stringent laws against libel and obscenity must be sacrificed for the longer-range goal of what is necessary and appropriate to maintain effective freedom of expression. This contemporary historical development is therefore a clear example of the dictum of Justice Benjamin N. Cardozo: "The tendency of a principle to expand itself to the limit of its logic may be counteracted by the tendency to confine itself within the limits of history. . . . Very often, the effect of history is to make the path of logic clear."[27]

We shall have a better understanding of what Justice Cardozo meant here if we take time to focus more closely upon the recent development of libel law. This particular history began in 1964 with the celebrated case, *New York Times* v. *Sullivan,* which has been described as "an opinion that may prove to be the best and the most important [the Court] has ever produced in the realm of freedom of speech."[28] L. B. Sullivan was Commissioner of Public Affairs in Montgomery, Alabama, at the time Martin Luther King, Jr., was involved in demonstrations on the campus of Alabama State Col-

lege. The *New York Times* printed a fund-raising advertisement for Dr. King containing some inaccurate statements about the commissioner and his role in these
demonstrations. Sullivan sued the *Times* for libel and
the Alabama courts awarded him $500,000 in damages.
The United States Supreme Court unanimously reversed these rulings, holding that the Alabama libel
laws did not meet the requirements of the First
Amendment. In a single paragraph of this opinion, as
Emerson says, "the wall of separation between libel and
the First Amendment came tumbling down."[29] Dispos-
ing of earlier Court statements that had placed libel
laws outside such protection, Justice Brennan asserted
that "libel can claim no talismanic immunity from constitutional limitations. It must be measured by standards that satisfy the First Amendment." These standards originate, he continued, in "a profound national
commitment to the principle that debate on public issues should be uninhibited, robust, and wide-open, and
that it may well include vehement, caustic, and sometimes unpleasantly sharp attacks on government and
public officials." Hence an advertisement such as that in
the *Times* on a major public question like civil rights
clearly qualifies for constitutional protection. The precise issue is "whether it forfeits this protection by the
falsity of some of its factual statements and by its al-
leged defamation."[30]

The rule of the Court on this issue was a historic
departure: false statements of fact *were* to be protected. Why? Because "erroneous statement is inevitable in free debate, and . . . must be protected if the
freedoms of expression are to have the 'breathing
space' that they 'need . . . to survive.'" To compel a
critic of official conduct to guarantee the truth of all his
factual statements under threat of a libel conviction
would inevitably lead to "self-censorship." Not only

would false speech be deterred: *all* criticism of official conduct would be deterred, "even though it is believed to be true and even though it is in fact true, because of doubt whether it can be proved in court or fear of the expense of having to do so." Such an approach "dampens the vigor and limits the variety of public debate." This protection is given, however, only up to a point. The press is not wholly at liberty to publish falsehoods damaging to an official's reputation. Such defamatory statements lose protection if the official can prove they were made with "actual malice," that is to say, "with knowledge that it was false or with reckless disregard of whether it was false or not." The Court then concluded that in Sullivan's case "the proof presented to show actual malice lacks the convincing clarity which the constitutional standard demands," and hence could not sustain a judgment in his favor.[31]

In this landmark case, then, the Court asserted that "the central meaning of the First Amendment" is to guarantee the right of citizens to criticize a public official. This is obviously not the whole meaning, since other freedoms are also protected, but it constitutes the core of speech protection.[32] If this right is not to be confined and hampered, then its exercise, which will often involve the defamation of officials, cannot be inhibited by the standard of truthfulness unless the falsehood is knowing and reckless. If we ask why the line should be drawn at the precise point of malice, we have the answer from Justice Brennan in another Court opinion that same year, 1964. "Calculated falsehood," he said, using the words of Justice Murphy we have already quoted, "falls into that class of utterances which 'are no essential part of any exposition of ideas, and are of such slight social value as a step to truth that any benefit that may be derived from them is clearly outweighed by the social interest in order and morality.' "[33] The Court has over the last decade held the line at this point. It even extended the *Times* ruling in 1967 to include "public figures."[34] Only if a person is neither a public official nor a public figure do statements about him cease to have constitutional protection. The reason, said the Court in 1974, is that private individuals have not voluntarily exposed themselves to risk of defamation, have less opportunity for rebuttal, and are much more vulnerable to injury than those in the public eye.[35]

What is the meaning of this sudden concern within the last decade to extend First Amendment protection to statements about public personalities?[36] One key is to be found in the civil rights controversy which formed the background of the *New York Times* case. Libel action was being used as a tool to silence attacks upon public officials by those in the civil rights movement, and the *Times* decision was obviously an attempt to protect this movement's apparatus of protest. The sensitivity of the Court here to sociological reality enabled such protest to maintain its dignity as political action and as a protest for redress of grievances.[37] Unless in these cases the base for exceptions to First Amendment values was exceedingly narrow, and positive commitment to these values exceedingly strong, restrictive forces would inevitably break through and suppression might become the rule. This is the concern eloquently voiced by Justice Hugo L. Black, speaking for the Court in 1966:

> The Constitution specifically selected the press . . . to play an important role in the discussion of public affairs. Thus the press serves and was designed to serve as a powerful antidote to any abuses of power by governmental officials and as a constitutionally chosen means for keeping officials selected by the people responsible to all the people whom they were elected to serve. Sup-

pression of the right of the press to praise or criticize
governmental agents and to clamor and contend for or
against change ... muzzles one of the very agencies the
Framers of our Constitution thoughtfully and deliberately selected to improve our society and keep it free.[38]

I said earlier that the Court's task is not simply to
adjudicate but to reconcile. Justice Black's remarks
spotlight the much more fundamental concern of the
Court in the libel cases, namely, that this reconciliation
is to be fostered not only between government and
individuals but also between government as one institution and the established press as another. What is to
be guaranteed is not simply freedom of expression on
the part of newspaper editors but, more precisely, freedom of the press. The separate clauses for each in the
First Amendment show that there is no redundancy
here. In the setting up of the three branches of government, the Founders' purpose was not to avoid friction
but, by reason of the inevitable friction, to accommodate power to freedom and vice versa, thereby saving
the people from autocracy. The guarantee of a free
press had an identical purpose: to create a fourth institution outside the government as an additional check
on the three official branches. The Constitution, in
other words, ordains an unruly contest between government and press without deciding the outcome. That
outcome depends upon the push and pull of all the
forces in society, since the contest is meant to serve the
public interest in the flow of news. The First Amendment weds this interest to the reporter's professional
interest, thereby throwing weight on the reporter's
side and away from government, since the underlying
assumption is that secrecy and control of news is all too
inviting and all too easily achieved.[39]

Hence what we have in the last decade is an effort of
the Court to go considerably beyond merely asserting

the importance of a neutral "marketplace for ideas." The concern of the members has rather been to protect the rights of the press as an institution even when it does *not* provide such a marketplace. In this they are in touch with a long tradition. "I deplore . . . the putrid state into which our newspapers have passed," complained Thomas Jefferson, "and the malignity, the vulgarity and mendacious spirit of those who write them. . . . It is however an evil for which there is no remedy, our liberty depends on freedom of the press, and that cannot be limited without being lost."[40] Newspapers and magazines have indeed been abusive, untruthful, and arrogant, but as Justice Byron R. White recently noted in a concurring opinion, "the balance struck by the First Amendment with respect to the press is that society must take the risk."[41] Our focus here has been on the taking of this risk by the gradual restriction of libel law in favor of more "breathing space" for press discussion of controversial public issues. But the Court took the same risk in 1974 when it said that no law can compel a newspaper to grant right of access for the reply of a political candidate it has criticized. Quality journalism may demand that a newspaper serve as a marketplace for debate at election time, but the First Amendment prohibits the government from mandating such responsibility.[42] And in the Pentagon Papers case in 1971 the Court asserted the constitutional right of the press to learn what it can and to publish whatever it learns, even when this involves allegedly stolen government documents. Only if there is clear evidence of immediate and catastrophic injury to the nation following directly from publication will a prior restraint be allowed.[43] The motive in all these decisions has been the same: to put the nation in touch with its own ideal, and to discern this ideal's meaning afresh in the pressing controversies of the day. Such an endeavor will always involve risk, because ultimately it is an attempt to articulate how best to live together as an ordered human community.

III

We have been considering the efforts of the Supreme Court over the last decade to articulate the American ideal of freedom of expression by specifying more exactly certain points at which First Amendment rights ended and other rights began. And we concluded that the ultimate concern of the Court in these areas seems to be not so much with the Free Speech Clause as with the Free Press Clause: the conviction that the well-being and freedom of our whole society is somehow intertwined with keeping the press independent of all government control. Our focus has thus been primarily on the First Amendment as a negative promotion of expression, the restriction of interference with that institution most charged with providing a "marketplace for ideas." Yet this cannot mean that the First Amendment has no positive side, that it cannot be used affirmatively to promote freedom of speech and press. For, as Meiklejohn has said, this constitutional guarantee is not primarily a device for winning new truth, although this is obviously important, but rather a device for sharing whatever truth has been won.[44] As early as 1945, Justice Black stated the importance of this affirmative duty of the government, and at the same time foreshadowed the thorny problems which have since developed from efforts to perform this duty:

> It would be strange indeed . . . if the grave concern for freedom of the press which prompted adoption of the First Amendment should be read as a command that the government was without power to protect that free-

dom. . . . That Amendment rests on the assumption that
the widest possible dissemination of information from
diverse and antagonistic sources is essential to the welfare of the public, that a free press is a condition of a free
society. Surely a command that the government itself
shall not impede the free flow of ideas does not afford
non-governmental combinations a refuge if they impose
restraints upon that constitutionally guaranteed freedom. Freedom to publish means freedom for all and not
for some. . . . Freedom of the press from governmental
interference under the First Amendment does not sanc-
tion repression of that freedom by private interests.[45]

Justice Black was speaking here in the context of antitrust legislation to eliminate monopoly and to increase
diversity in press coverage. This type of government
control, by which public interest, as embodied in the
antitrust laws, overrides First Amendment claims of
the media, has never raised serious problems. The reason is that the government is here using its commerce
power to advance a social objective which is outside the
system of free expression. The difficulty arises, as we
shall see, when the affirmative measure in question
aims to expose deficiencies within the system itself in
order to make it work better.

Both Jerome Barron and Thomas Emerson have expressed deep concern with these deficiencies. The former has eloquently underlined what he calls the irony
of the *New York Times* v. *Sullivan* case, namely, the
unexamined assumption that reducing newspaper ex-
posure to libel litigation will remove restraints on expression and ensure an informed society. He terms such
an assumption "the romantic view of the First Amendment," since it equates protecting the right with providing for it, and totally ignores the power of the mass
media to suppress information. Whereas the crucial
concern today should be not only to guarantee the exis-

tence of public forums for discussion but also to guarantee access to them. Freedom of media content should not be confused with freedom to restrict access. To do so is to confer upon the media the very censorship role denied to the government.[46] Emerson is equally concerned. Search for the truth is handicapped, he says, because much of the argument is never heard or heard only weakly. Political decisions tend to become distorted because feedback to the government is feeble. The system is, moreover, choked with a bland and conventional wisdom, and this works toward shielding the existing order and inhibiting social change. He readily concedes that grave administrative and procedural problems immediately arise from any affirmative interference by government in this area, but he believes that there is no alternative. "The weaknesses of the existing system are so profound that failure to act is the more dangerous course."[47]

Emerson adds, however, a strong caveat. Certain limited forms of control may indeed make the system work better, but such controls cannot be imposed on any broad scale without destroying the system altogether. Ultimately the reason is that government would then be exercising the right to determine the value of particular forms of expression; but the more immediate reason is that the very presence of government, with apparatus for investigating and enforcing, is itself inhibiting and repressive. Hence any regulation at all is dangerous, and can be tolerated only under the most exceptional circumstances.[48] This is an echo of what Justice Brandeis once said: "Experience should teach us to be most on our guard to protect liberty when the Government's purposes are beneficent. . . . The greatest dangers to liberty lurk in insidious encroachment by men of zeal, well-meaning but without understanding."[49] And more recently Justice Black has pointed out that the motives behind a particular state law may have been to do good, but history "indicates that urges to do good have led to the burning of books and even to the burning of 'witches.' "[50] Hence once more the Supreme Court must become involved with gamble and risk in its effort to interpret the First Amendment for twentieth-century America, the challenge now coming not from the need to protect the exercise of free expression but from the need to purify it.

This involvement of the Court has taken place, for better or worse, not in the domain of the print press but in that of the electronic press. The reason is that government regulation has permeated this field ever since the Radio Act of 1927, justified by the "exceptional circumstances" of which Emerson speaks. These are the physical characteristics inherent in the medium itself: the electromagnetic spectrum can accommodate only so many potential broadcasters. It is as if there were a permanent scarcity of printing presses that could turn out only so many newspapers.[51] Practical experience in the early days of radio made it clear that traditional laissez-faire policy would lead to chaos; with everyone on the air, no one could be heard; effective communication was being destroyed and basic First Amendment goals frustrated. Hence a system of government licensing was adopted which led eventually to the Communications Act of 1934 and the establishment of the Federal Communications Commission. This power of the Commission to choose among applicants "is not a denial of free speech," said the Court in 1943, since the First Amendment does not include "the right to use the facilities of radio without a license." Nor does the Communications Act "restrict the Commission merely to supervision of the traffic. It puts upon the Commission the burden of determining the composition of the traffic."[52] Because broadcasters were to be few in number and were to be in some sense trustees of the government, they were not to be permitted so to pursue their private interests that they could neglect to serve and inform the public. The limitation of private rights of access must not endanger the public's right of access to a robust marketplace of ideas. Government regulation over the years has therefore not been limited to matters of electromagnetic engineering; it has also involved a certain control over the content of broadcasting, justified by the so-called fairness doctrine.

Formalized first in a 1949 FCC report and given statutory recognition in a 1959 amendment of the Communications Act,[53] the fairness doctrine is a very general public interest policy that asks licensees to devote a reasonable amount of program time to controversial issues of the day, and to do so fairly by affording a reasonable opportunity for contrasting viewpoints to be voiced on these issues. It is the enforcement of the second provision of this doctrine which allows government some control over the news and public affairs programming of radio and television. The crucial question, of course, is how much control should the government have? Traditional First Amendment theory would say that there should be no control at all over the content of journalism. Does the fairness doctrine mean, then, that the rights of broadcast journalists can be abridged, whereas those of other journalists cannot? The Supreme Court had to face this dilemma in 1969 in the now famous case, *Red Lion Broadcasting Co.* v. *FCC.* The issue was whether someone who felt his character had been maligned on the air could demand that the station give him free time to respond. The unanimous decision was that he could. The station had to yield its freedom in order to enhance the public's right

to be informed; the rights of the broadcaster under the
First Amendment were "abridgeable" and had to be
balanced with the rights of the general public.

What we are involved with in *Red Lion*, then, is
clearly an evolution of principle in the First Amendment area. In upholding the fairness doctrine's personal attack rule, the Court went well beyond the scarcity rationale of its 1943 decision. The focus of this 1969
opinion, written by Justice Byron White, was on the
First Amendment "right of the viewers and listeners,
not the right of the broadcasters. . . . It is the right of
the public to receive suitable access to social, political,
aesthetic, moral, and other ideas and experiences
which is crucial here." Those who are licensed, he said,
"stand no better than those to whom licenses are
refused. A license permits broadcasting, but the licensee has no constitutional right to be the one who holds
the license or to monopolize a radio frequency to the
exclusion of his fellow citizens." The fairness doctrine
may therefore require a licensee "to share his frequency with others and to conduct himself as a proxy
or fiduciary with obligations to present those views and
voices which are representative of his community."
The government may therefore certainly condition the
granting or renewal of a license on a willingness to
present such views. Nor is there any inconsistency here
with "constitutional provisions forbidding abridgment
of freedom of speech and freedom of the press."[54] On
the contrary, the Court seemed to be saying, the reach
of the First Amendment is itself conditioned by the
public character of radio and television as well as by the
extent of government involvement therein. The licensee, on such a theory, is an agent of the government, a
proxy, and has no First Amendment rights of his own
(except for his own expression). "The First Amendment
right would run from the individual or group seeking

to engage in expression, or seeking to listen, to the
government; not from the licensee (except as to his own
expression) to the government."[55] Hence licensees
would be subject to controls while users and listeners
would not.

Red Lion was strong medicine for broadcasters who
obstinately clung to their position that the electronic
press was no different from the print press, and that
consequently they, in their capacity as editors, should
enjoy the same First Amendment protection. Their argument was that the actual effect of the fairness doctrine was to inhibit and restrict broadcast journalism,
thereby reducing coverage of controversial issues and
inevitably leading to self-censorship. To ensure a balanced presentation, in other words, was to ensure no
vigorous presentation at all; controversial viewpoints
would simply be screened out in favor of a dreary
blandness. Justice White acknowledged in his opinion
that this possibility of a "chilling effect" was a "serious
matter," but he then dismissed it as "at best specula-
tive." If licensees "should suddenly prove timorous," he
added, "the Commission is not powerless to insure that
they give adequate and fair attention to public issues."[56] The Court pursued the objection no further at
the time, but since then it has developed into the crucial issue. It raises the whole question of the *scope* of
First Amendment impact upon broadcasting, and also
highlights the uncertainty of the law's present response. In the last few years ample evidence has been
found to show that in fact the FCC exerts an enormous
chilling power over electronic media.[57] Even when
there is no direct influence, there is still that censorship
of the "lifted eyebrow," to use Julian Goodman's
phrase, which creates an atmosphere of surveillance
which can easily become destructive of journalists'
morale. Obvious examples of such surveillance are the

pre-Watergate efforts of the Nixon Administration to politicize broadcasting by influencing program content.[58]

The fairness doctrine can therefore be taken too far or applied too rigidly by petty public officials who are the perennial bane of bureaucracies. *Red Lion* opposed such misuse, and is clearly an instance of the doctrine's invocation to implement debate rather than to retard it.[59] But the danger stood out in bold relief once again in the controversy leading up to the Court's important 1973 decision in *Columbia Broadcasting System* v. *Democratic National Committee.* In *Red Lion* the Court found the First Amendment to lie in the right of the public to hear, but said nothing about the further question of whether the ordinary citizen had any right to use the electronic press to speak. The issue was joined when both the Democratic National Committee and an antiwar group, Business Executives Move for Peace, sought to purchase reply time on the air to respond to statements and policies of the Nixon Administration. The demands at first sight seemed to advance First Amendment principles, since no President had ever been granted more free air time than Richard Nixon, and to oblige stations to broadcast replies by those personally affected by Nixon programs appeared to guarantee a collision of genuine advocates. The question, then, was whether the First Amendment embodied the right of someone to express his own views, in his own way, by buying advertising time on the air. Was the self-fulfillment of the individual speaker to be paramount here, or were broadcasters to have the right to decide who speaks on their stations and who does not?[60]

An intermediate court ruled in favor of the speaker,[61] but the Supreme Court reversed by a vote of seven to two. In an opinion written by Chief Justice

Warren E. Burger, the Court reaffirmed the principle
that scarcity requires the electronic press to be tested
differently from the print press, but added that this is
not a principle without bounds, that not all regulation
can be justified in the name of scarcity. Overzealous
invocation of rules such as the fairness doctrine could
cause an "erosion of the journalistic discretion of broadcasters in the coverage of public issues." Yet it is upon
this discretion of the licensee that the successful opera-
tion of the doctrine must primarily depend. Hence no
private individual or group has a right to command the
use of broadcast facilities. The choice of who should
speak on public issues has to be made by broadcasters
whose function is to inform, and not by bureaucrats
whose function is to regulate. To extend the public's
constitutional right to the purchase of advertising time
would lead to an "undesirable" enlargement of governmental control over the content of broadcasting. The
Court then spoke once again, as so often before, in
terms of commitment and risk:

> For better or worse editing is what editors are for; and
> editing is selection and choice of material. That editors
> —newspaper or broadcast—can and do abuse this
> power is beyond doubt, but that is not reason to deny
> the discretion Congress provided. Calculated risks of
> abuse are taken in order to preserve higher values. The
> presence of these risks is nothing new; the authors of the
> Bill of Rights accepted the reality that these risks were
> evils for which there was no acceptable remedy other
> than a spirit of moderation and a sense of responsibility
> —and civility—on the part of those who exercise the
> guaranteed freedom of expression.[62]

Columbia Broadcasting thus became a significant clar-
ification of *Red Lion:* a recognition that, besides the
First Amendment rights of the citizen as viewer and
listener, there are also the rights of the broadcaster, not

only as to his own expression, but more importantly as to his editorial prerogatives. "If we must choose whether editorial decisions are to be made in the free judgment of individual broadcasters, or imposed by bureaucratic fiat, the choice must be for freedom."[63]

Both of these important cases would seem at first sight to be grappling only with the complex legal question of how the exercise of freedom of expression may be affirmatively promoted in the electronic press, within present licensing requirements, without leaving broadcasters at the mercy of government personnel. But there is a much deeper reason for the evolution in First Amendment theory now taking place in broadcasting. This is the conviction which the public at large has of the power of radio and television. Here ultimately is the key to the different treatment accorded by the Supreme Court to newspapers and broadcasters. This is not a constitutional argument; indeed, one could effectively argue in the opposite direction, that the medium's greater power requires greater protection from government interference.[64] Yet this is not the feeling of people generally. They are not in fact put off by the idea of a free market and self-determination for newspaper editors, but with the electronic press they are more comfortable with the present policy of limited surveillance.[65] For the broadcast industry, in terms of both numbers reached and visual effect, has become the most efficient marketplace of ideas ever devised. Studies have shown that 67 percent of Americans prefer the electronic media to other sources of information, and are also more apt to believe a story they get from radio or television. The result is that the impact, and audience, of the nightly news is far greater than any one newspaper or magazine. Moreover, approximately 95 percent of American homes contain at least one television set, and that set is turned on for an average of nearly six hours every day.[66] Hence in supporting the policy of limited surveillance the Supreme Court is responding to a need and desire in society as a whole. The gamble this time, however, is that such surveillance in the end will not restrict expression but promote it, by encouraging those who wish to speak and providing increased coverage and diversity for those who wish to hear.

IV

My approach to the First Amendment has been to deal with it as a commitment to a certain mode of being human in civil society, to a certain value system. The three levels of treatment I have followed made it clear that there are serious obstacles today to internalizing our ideal of freedom of expression. In order to overcome these obstacles and to apply the tradition in concrete situations, the Supreme Court must somehow fuse myth and reason, inching its way through the complexity of individual cases toward a newly clarified sense of direction and goal. This procedure will always require some balancing of rights and duties, some accommodation to both freedom and control. "The great antinomies of life," says Robert Bellah, "are never solved by grasping one polarity and forgetting the other. Our problem is not to get rid of control in any absolute sense but to find a new kind of control that will allow a wider freedom."[67] How much social control is permitted over expression? How much restraint can there be on the individual before commitment to the ideal is diminished in the community?

Alexander Bickel has wisely observed that law can never make us as secure as we are when we do not need it. In this perspective the First Amendment freedom was most secure during those years when it was neither challenged nor defined. Bickel was speaking here in the context of the Pentagon Papers case which he argued before the Supreme Court in 1971. The American press was freer, he claims, before it won than after its victory, since no previous attempt had ever been made by government to censor a newspaper by seeking to impose restraint prior to publication. Once that step was taken, freedom was in a sense diminished.[68] The reason, I would presume, although Bickel does not elaborate the point, is that law is society's response to disorder, and to invoke a guarantee never before invoked means that new disorder has arisen, a new threat which earlier did not exist and which must now be watched and kept under control. Unfortunately the shift presently taking place from a laissez-faire culture to one of mass technology must inevitably bring disorder. Such a transition period will always give rise to temptation to control too much, to use too much power. It would be surprising if such technological advance did not result in a certain loss of perspective in society as a whole. New problems arising from the exercise of freedom of expression have therefore to be seen as part of this larger canvas of social changes.

But the question for the Supreme Court in the First Amendment area is how to deal concretely with such problems. This is a momentous task, one of creatively adapting an inherited institution to meet the twentieth-century crisis of freedom and order insofar as this crisis impinges upon an American ideal. It is not easy. Our problem is the totalitarian tendency of the democratic faith itself, gravitating as it does toward the opposite evils of intolerance or of indifference; yielding either to the tyranny of ideas or to the emptiness of politics without ideas.[69] The First Amendment thus enjoins us to guard the marketplace of ideas but not wholly to place our trust in it. This marketplace is precisely the measure of our freedom. But the majority rule to which it gives rise must be watched, and the

Supreme Court has been constituted as agency of this watchfulness.

I have been speaking all along about faith in the human. Let me end with a word about faith in the superhuman. For the only real safeguard against dangers from the majority principle is the conviction that under God truth and right are not matters of majority vote. Democracy without faith in God is therefore much more likely to sink into mob rule. Only if one believes that majority opinion does not determine truth, will it become paramount to keep open all the channels of communication so that every minority will have the chance to become a majority through persuasion. The Christian basis for this view is, of course, that the workings of God's Spirit cannot be predicted nor its voice stilled by any human contrivance. Faith in God is thus a support for the First Amendment as a procedure, as a faith in certain means to achieve an ideal.[70] In his inaugural address, Lyndon Johnson caught something of this relationship between faith in the human and faith in the divine, and his remarks highlight the type of risk which we as a nation take when we guarantee the freedoms of the First Amendment:

> We have no promise from God that our greatness will endure. We have been allowed by him to seek greatness with the sweat of our hands and the strength of our spirit.
> . . .
> If we fail now, then we have forgotten . . . that democracy rests on faith, that freedom asks more than it gives, and the judgment of God is harshest on those who are most favored.
> If we succeed, it will not be because of what we have, but it will be because of what we are; not because of what we own, but rather because of what we believe.
> For we are a nation of believers.[71]

4

THE CHURCHES
IN A PLURALISTIC LAND

Witness to Mystery and Justice
as a Public Trust

The Free Speech and Free Press Clauses of the First Amendment represent, as we have seen, an act of faith in a certain mode of being human in civil society. They are thus part of a larger national commitment both to the capacity of people to rule themselves and to the judicious limitation of government power. In this chapter I shall focus on the religion clauses of the First Amendment and emphasize that they are no less an act of faith and no less a part of this larger national commitment. When they first became law in 1791, the No Establishment and Free Exercise Clauses constituted a relationship between the churches and government which was unique in the world of the time, an achievement of political intelligence which was to have momentous consequences. One historian has said that, "on the administration side, the two most profound revolutions which have occurred in the entire history of the church have been these: first, the change of the church, in the fourth century, from a voluntary society . . . to a society conceived as necessarily coextensive with the civil community and endowed with the power to enforce the adherence of all members of the civil community; second, the reversal of this change . . . in America."[1]

This reversal had been carefully scrutinized and discussed long before it was codified into law. Initially it was thought of as an experiment with a very important structure of civil society: institutional religion. As such it involved risk, for a religion mediates the values and ideals of a society just as effectively as do institutions that are political, economic, or educational. This risk involved a threefold belief, a threefold act of faith, if you will: in religious pluralism, in religious freedom, and in the importance of religious witness. In what follows I analyze each of these in turn.

Before we begin, however, let me make one important observation. To designate our general discussion area as that of church and state can be misleading. The problem as it exists in America is not so much a relationship between two institutions as one between two outlooks of the individual, his outlook as citizen and his outlook as member of a religious denomination. In a democracy, where sovereignty resides in the people, the struggle between God and Caesar must necessarily be internalized. To project it outward, to deal with it as wholly objective, is to miss its key dimension. What we are really dealing with in America is a competition between two religions, the one civil, the other denominational. It is up to the individual citizen to balance these two sets of claims, to decide upon the extent of his allegiance to each.[2] Historically, as we have seen, our nation has attempted through its ideals and goals to bind the people together under God, giving them, however unsuccessfully at times, a genuine apprehension of his transcendent reality. Americans have thus tended to find the symbols of ultimate meaning not only in their churches but also in their country. Hence the so-called conflict between church and state is basically an attempt by citizens with allegiance to both institutions to evaluate and criticize the one by criteria received from the other. We should not be surprised, then, to find tensions in this area which are perennial, built as they are into the whole fabric of our society. With this important observation as preamble, let us turn now to the first of the three beliefs I just mentioned, namely, our commitment to religious pluralism.

I

Religious pluralism was a fact in America long before it became an object of belief. This was not because the various religious bodies which took root in the colonies were particularly tolerant of each other. On the contrary, they all seem to have behaved in what came later to be called "typical sectarian fashion," each one claiming exclusively to be "the Church," and absolutizing those particularities in doctrine and practice which distinguished it from other Christian groups. The reason there was at the same time so much religious freedom in the colonies was chiefly due to the openness and sparsely settled nature of the country: the nonconformist simply moved away into that vast space where his deviance immediately became orthodoxy. Groups holding divergent and incompatible views on religious questions thus gradually came to coexist in different parts of the country. As a sense of national community grew, giving birth to political consensus in resistance to Great Britain, disagreement on things religious came to be regarded as less and less important. The two principal movements in American Christianity at the time, moreover, rationalism and pietism, tended to encourage this growing belief that formal differences in doctrine and worship were not of ultimate importance. Rationalists like Franklin and Jefferson believed that the essentials of any religion could be reduced to a common set of intellectual propositions regarding God, immortality, and the life of virtue. Pietists, on the other hand, in the tradition of John Wesley, were convinced that spiritual nourishment had to be found in experience, not in the barren intellectualism of creeds, doctrine, and theology. Thus rationalists appealed to the head and pietists to the heart to reach the same conclusion at the very time that, for geographic reasons, many different sects were enjoying relatively peaceful coexistence.[3]

This de facto pluralism meant that none of the dominant churches was in a position to press for religious uniformity. Indeed, there was a practical necessity for all of them to connive at religious variety; because no single church could make a successful bid for national establishment, it was to the self-interest of each to be tolerant of all in order to guarantee such toleration for itself. The motivation was thus purely pragmatic; very few church pronouncements at the time articulated any positive ideological thrust for toleration. Churches did not really contribute to religious liberty. All the evidence says that "they stumbled into it, they were compelled into it, they accepted it at last because they had to, or because they saw its strategic value."[4] This de facto pluralism likewise made one other conclusion unavoidable: since so many sects, holding very different beliefs, were able to coexist in peace, it followed that uniformity of religious practice was obviously not essential to the public welfare, something hitherto assumed to be true for centuries by all the countries of Western Europe. It was this last realization, that religious solidarity was not needed to stabilize the social order, which paved the way for the No Establishment and Free Exercise Clauses of the First Amendment.

"Congress shall make no law respecting an establishment of religion, or prohibiting the free exercise thereof." These clauses did not create a new idea, but were rather the legal recognition of an actual state of things which had come to be seen as practically unavoidable. The Founders wanted to formulate a principle that would guarantee the participation of all churches in the common social unity of the republic, while at the same time not compromising those distinctive modes of worship and belief proper to each. The First Amendment was therefore conceived to be an experiment in the political realm, an effort to strengthen the new nation by excluding from government concern all religious differences among its people. At the time it was by no means certain that the experiment would be successful, that is to say, that it would necessarily be conducive to public peace and order. Writing in 1785, six years before the Amendment's adoption, Jefferson reminded his state of Virginia that the states of Pennsylvania and New York had long had an official policy of no establishment. "The experiment was new and doubtful when they made it," he said. "It has answered beyond conception. They flourish infinitely. Religion is well supported; of various kinds, indeed, but all good enough; all sufficient to preserve peace and order."[5] Speaking on this same question in 1808, seventeen years after the Amendment's adoption, Jefferson could say: "We have solved by fair experiment, the great and interesting question whether freedom of religion is compatible with order in government, and obedience to the laws."[6] Somewhere within the twenty-three-year period between these two statements, then, an ideological revolution took place which finally made the experiment of religious pluralism acceptable in theory as well as in practice. What was responsible for this ideological shift?

According to Sidney Mead it was generally recognized at the time that establishments in other countries rested on two basic assumptions: first, that the well-being of society depended upon a body of shared religious beliefs—the nature of man, his place in the cosmos, his destiny, and his conduct toward his fellowmen —and second, that the only way to guarantee the inculcation of these necessary beliefs was to put the coercive power of the state behind the institution responsible for their inculcation. Now what gradually became clear to statesmen and clergy alike was that acceptance of religious pluralism meant giving up not the first assumption but only the second, namely, that the state must use its coercive power to inculcate religious belief. The essence of the ideological shift was therefore the rejection of coercion in favor of persuasion. With the exception of a few extreme deists and agnostics, the Founders never interpreted the principle of uncoerced consent to mean that government ought to be indifferent to religion, since from religion came truths essential for public order and stability. The principle meant rather that responsibility for inculcating these truths, thought to be common to every religion, rested with the churches alone, to be carried out in whatever ways individual churches wished, relying upon persuasion, however, and not upon the government's coercive power. We should note too that this ideological shift was in many ways the natural extension into the religious sphere of the eighteenth century's key idea that free consent was the only rational basis for organizing civil government. The two movements we mentioned earlier, for example, rationalism and pietism, both wanted to promote this extension, though for very different reasons: the one basing autonomy in religious matters upon the primacy of reason in weighing evidence, the other, upon the direct guidance of the Holy Spirit and the reading of sacred Scripture.[7]

In any event, all the Protestant churches gradually came to accept this ideology for pluralism, reformulating it to fit their respective traditions which originally (with the exception of the Baptists) contained little or no theoretical justification for it. Pluralism was eventually justified as a new outward manifestation of traditional Protestant anti-authoritarianism, fostering anew traditional Protestant virtues of voluntarism and privatism. One far-reaching result of this reformulation was a new organizational form for Protestant churches. They began to think of themselves eventually as "denominations," groups that neither claimed to be exclusively "the Church" nor absolutized the peculiarities that distinguished them from other groups. Unlike a sect, a denomination recognized itself as a finite witness to the Christian gospel, imperfect in knowledge and authority as well as in practice; hence the abiding fragmentation we find in American Protestantism, as well as its more or less negative conception of the state. Henceforth, it was thought, the state could never become involved in any way in the religious sphere without immediately threatening the free church system either by patronizing some churches or by coercing all.[8]

Jews and Roman Catholics were not unaffected by this nineteenth-century rationalization of religious pluralism. American Jews tended to view their society and culture both then and later as "ambiguous mixtures of secularism and Christianity."[9] They have generally preferred strong religious pluralism and strict government neutrality not from some ideology of church-state relations but from their experience of Jewish history. They know that whenever a government has been supportive of one or another Christian church in the past, Jews have invariably had to put up with some discomfort, and not infrequently with much worse. Such supportive relationships usually involve at least some intolerance toward religious minorities, precisely because the importance of religious differences is thereby increased. Jews have learned from bitter experience that it is wise to minimize these differences.[10] Hence in America, with the possible exception of Orthodox Jews, they have traditionally given strong support to Protestant voluntarism and privatism, even though Judaism itself is the most normative of religions.

Like Jews, Roman Catholics were a very small minority when religious pluralism was being given its ideological underpinning. Unlike Jews, however, Catholics could not accept the militant privatism of the Protestant denominations, because their tradition has consistently favored cooperative arrangements between governments and religious groups. For a Catholic, government ought to have an interest in the relationship of its citizens to God. Mutually advantageous arrangements should therefore be worked out pragmatically. This ought to be especially true in the United States, where the sovereignty of God in human life has always been publicly recognized. Hence the Catholic position is that the pluralism guaranteed by the First Amendment cannot be understood to assert or imply that the nature of a religious organization is such that it inherently demands the most absolute separation of church and state. Cooperation may never become actual but it must indeed be possible, albeit on a nondiscriminatory basis. John Courtney Murray used to say that in one sense it is irrelevant what the Founders originally thought about such cooperation. "What is in question is the meaning and content of the first of our American prejudices, not its genesis." The Catholic "rejects the notion that any of these sectarian theses enter into the content or implications of the First Amendment in such wise as to demand the assent of all American citizens. If this were the case, the very article that bars any establishment of religion would somehow establish one."[11]

These reactions of Christians and Jews to the First Amendment show that, although all have welcomed in practice the guarantees of free exercise and no establishment, each tradition has had its problems vis-à-vis the others in integrating the Amendment into its own history. In fact, one aspect of the original ideological shift has never been adequately integrated. Sidney Mead calls it the Trojan horse in the citadel of religious pluralism. The dilemma stems from the fact that the legal and political forms of this pluralism were worked out not by the clergy but by statesmen who by and large were disciples of the Enlightenment. As we saw earlier, these statesmen believed that churches (or "sects" as they usually called them) should flourish in America because it was important for the general welfare. That is to say, they believed that all churches held and taught in common the "essentials of every religion," and that these essentials were not only relevant but vital for the health of the nation. This implied, of course, that what was not commonly held was neither relevant nor vital. Whatever a religious group might hold as a peculiar tenet of its own faith, which made it distinct from other groups and constituted the reason for its separate existence, was thought to be at best only of indirect value to the republic. Hence "all the spectacular success of the free churches in America in effecting numerical growth and geographic expansion ... has taken place under this Damoclean sword—the haunting suspicion that somehow relevance to the general welfare decreased in proportion to sectarian success."[12]

This Damoclean sword has had some very far-reaching consequences for the churches in this pluralistic land. Spiritual compartmentalization is one consequence, noted even in the last century by Alexis de Tocqueville. Speaking specifically of Roman Catholics, he said that they "have divided the intellectual world

into two parts: in the one they place the doctrines of
revealed religion, which they assent to without discussion; in the other they leave those political truths which
they believe the Deity has left open to free inquiry.
Thus the Catholics of the United States are at the same
time the most submissive believers and the most independent citizens."[13] A second consequence is the one
we have discussed previously, namely, the phenomenon known as civil religion: insofar as individual
denominations have relinquished their claims to be
"the Church," the nation itself has tended more and
more to assume this function, speaking with far greater
authority than purely voluntary ecclesiastical societies.
The third consequence, however, is the most serious:
the churches have become confused in regard to what
should be their primary religious witness in a pluralistic
land. This is the question that will occupy us shortly.
But in order to deal with it in proper perspective I
think we ought first examine in some detail how the
country spelled out concretely its commitment to religious pluralism, namely, by a commitment to religious
freedom.

II

Religious freedom in America must be seen as an
extension of religious pluralism. At the start of its history our country embraced in practice and theory a
policy of government neutrality in regard to religion.
Both statesmen and clergy came to believe, although as
we saw for very different reasons, that this was a much
better way to secure peace and order in the young
republic than by government involvement. The No Establishment and Free Exercise Clauses were therefore
understood to prescribe a mutual independence: religion was to be safeguarded from the power of the state,

and political society was to be safeguarded from interference by organized religion. For the first time in the memory of the West a nation's churches were to be insulated from the intervention of its government, whether this intervention be used to establish religion or to restrain its practice. The gain for the churches was, of course, an increase in their freedom. But there was gain for the state as well, namely, the avoidance of political strife along religious lines, since common experience made it clear that whenever religion becomes a political issue, it invariably exhibits qualities that are both explosive and divisive. Government neutrality thus set limits to those absolutist tendencies endemic to every church, preventing any single one from becoming a monopoly and imposing its particular form on the people. Here in America the state could neither restrict nor become captive to any religious vision, yet each religious vision could flourish and expand insofar as it relied upon persuasion and not upon force. In claiming freedom for themselves, religious groups would have to affirm equal freedom for others, whatever their beliefs might be.

I said at the start that these religion clauses were an extraordinary achievement of political intelligence, and so they were. The leitmotiv running through the process of their adoption was the American impulse toward freedom, both political and religious. This impulse brought an emphatic reaffirmation of the distinction between the religious and political orders, a distinction quite common in medieval Christendom, but almost completely lost to Europe through the rise of national monarchies and the development of royal absolutism. One reason Americans embraced the distinction so strongly was that they inherited it through English common law, where it had somehow managed to survive. But the chief reason was its power to allay the fears of statesmen like James Madison and Thomas Jefferson that too much church would corrupt the state, and the fears of ministers like Roger Williams that too much state would corrupt the church. Such fears made both groups eager to deny to government any competence in the field of religion and to establish freedom in this area as the rule. They therefore pressed the distinction between spiritual and temporal—to an exaggerated degree perhaps, but, as John Courtney Murray once said, government rarely appears to better advantage than when passing self-denying ordinances. In any event, everyone then and since has agreed that exaggerating the distinction is a danger much to be preferred to its abolition.[14]

The view I have just sketched of religious freedom makes for a very idyllic picture indeed. The single function of government in its neutral stance is to see to it that the guarantee of this freedom is effective. Yet the most complex historical and legal difficulties have arisen whenever government has sought to exercise this function. The reason is that the Founders never spelled out precisely *how* such religious freedom was to be guaranteed. Some say that they were deliberately ambiguous, either because they themselves could not agree, or because they saw a positive advantage in leaving the question open for future generations. If so, then they succeeded. The question is indeed open, many arguing that the best way to guarantee religious freedom is to make the distinction between church and state as complete as humanly possible, "thus building up a wall of separation" between the two. This wall metaphor was used almost casually by Thomas Jefferson in an 1802 letter to the Baptist Association of Danbury, Connecticut, yet it has had, as we shall see, some fateful consequences for the interpretation of the First Amendment.[15]

A very different metaphor was chosen by James Madison, who spoke thirty years later about "the line of separation between the rights of religion and Civil authority."[16] The image of a "line" has the advantage of being much more flexible than that of a "wall," its elements constantly changing so as to make it difficult, as Madison noted, to trace with such distinctness as to avoid collisions and doubts. Hence it does not conjure up a confrontation between two antagonistic institutions, separated for all time by an impregnable barrier that must be defended by one and attacked by the other. Madison's metaphor makes it much easier to see that what is really the case is that Americans, who in fact belong as individuals to both institutions, are engaged in a common quest to determine where the line is to be drawn at any particular point in the nation's history.

This is the approach advanced by the late Wilber G. Katz of the University of Chicago Law School. "Except for occasional flights of rhetoric," wrote Katz, "no one contends either that absolute separation of church and state is required by the First Amendment or that such a rule would be desirable." The reason is that the concept of separation does not provide its own principle of limitation. "In determining the limits of constitutional separation, it is the concept of religious freedom which provides the criterion. The principle of church-state separation is an instrumental principle." In other words, separation *ordinarily* promotes religious freedom, and is defensible only so long as it does so. This promotion of religious freedom must be carefully distinguished from the promotion of religious belief. The favorite example of Katz is the chaplaincy program in the armed services. Strict church-state separation would mean the elimination of this program, thereby seriously limiting the free exercise of religion by mak-

ing it impossible to provide opportunities for worship
and instruction. Even though such a policy would have
the great advantage of relieving the military of some
highly embarrassing problems involving establishment
of religious categories and the apportionment of facilities, it has never been followed or even advocated.
Consequently the principle of full government neutrality does not require that the state become an adversary
to religion. As in the case of the armed services, the
state may do a great deal which appears superficially to
aid religion. "It may do these things, not because im-
partial aid to religion or encouragement of religion is an
appropriate object of government, but because insistence upon strict separation would limit religious freedom and would thus violate neutrality."[17] Government
neutrality aims therefore at maximizing religious freedom and requires only that degree of separation which
is compatible with maximum freedom.[18]

This approach of Professor Katz is theoretical and
abstract, and as an interpretation of recent decisions of
the Supreme Court, it is debatable. The Court is always
dealing with concrete, justiciable controversies between parties arguing against each other through
elaborately defined legal procedures. In such situations
the Court has to distinguish as carefully as possible between what promotes religious freedom and what promotes religious belief, and this is never easy. Hence it
is not at all surprising that the Justices seem to entertain
different views of the First Amendment at different
times.[19] To focus now upon any one of these cases
would be somewhat tedious and not to our purpose.
Suffice it to say that they all represent efforts to fix the
boundary at which conflicting interests balance. This
"cannot be determined by any general formula in advance," wrote Justice Holmes in 1903, "but points in
the line, or helping to establish it, are fixed by decisions

that this or that concrete case falls on the nearer or farther side."[20] We have here an echo of Madison's "line of separation" between church and state: Supreme Court decisions are not like large stones mortared into a solid wall, but like temporary points where the line appears to the majority of Justices to be at the moment.[21]

Nevertheless, the line at any given time is always drawn, and just now we can verbalize it as follows: the First Amendment guarantees to all religious groups freedom from government restraint and discrimination, but at the same time it also guarantees them freedom from government aid, even when this is offered without discrimination.[22] The Court's insistence on this last guarantee has become the neuralgic issue of church-state relations over the last thirty years, especially as these have centered on the question of nondiscriminatory aid to religious schools. Many jurists have stoutly defended the use of public funds for religious schools by arguing that such funding would be a means of promoting, not religion, but precisely religious freedom, that is to say, the freedom of religious choice. The burden of sharing the enormous cost of public education, properly assessed upon all taxpayers, greatly reduces the practical freedom to choose a school not supported by public funds. Not to lift this restraint is to discriminate against religious schools precisely because they are religious, thereby greatly weakening the force of the Free Exercise Clause.[23]

The Supreme Court has thus far not been sympathetic to this line of argument. But it is important to recognize that this is not because the Justices believe that the argument makes no sense (since it is obviously the basis for financial aid in other countries) nor because they believe religion to be a private affair of no concern to the state. "We are a religious people whose institutions presuppose a Supreme Being." Justice William O. Douglas wrote these words in a notable decision,[24] and Justice Harlan underlined them when he spoke at another time of those "many areas in which the pervasive activities of the State justify some special provision for religion to prevent it from being submerged in an all embracing secularism."[25] Why then is nondiscriminatory aid to religion not a viable interpretation of the First Amendment? The reason is that it meets at present so much opposition in American society from those who favor a very strict separationist policy. These obviously include secular humanists, who believe that their presuppositions provide just as strong a basis for loyalty to country as belief in a Supreme Being, and who consequently seek themselves to be free from government pressure in favor of religion. But also included are the Protestant and Jewish groups of whom we already spoke, who want strict government neutrality in this area because nondiscriminatory aid to religious schools would inevitably discriminate in its allocation in favor of the large Catholic school system, thereby tending to promote political division along religious lines, the very thing the Founders wanted to avoid.

Over the years the majority of the Justices have preferred this interpretation, even at the risk of some inconsistency in the First Amendment area. Were they to do otherwise, they would be opposing the values of a highly articulate constituency representing the majority of American citizens, and they would be doing so in an area where history is at best cloudy and precedent slim. Richard Morgan has well summarized their situation: "The Supreme Court may be able, indeed, it may be one of its important functions, to set the pace of national policy change from time to time. But there are limits. For the Court to attempt to swim across powerfully moving tides in search of doctrinal consistency would be to risk the long-run political position of the institution just as surely as continued slighting of the value of doctrinal consistency would risk that position. Constitutional 'principles' are meaningless unless the values they are meant to serve are made explicit, and the whole attempt is bootless if the values are not widely shared."[26] In other words, the line separating the promotion of religious belief from the promotion of religious freedom is going to remain rather jagged for some time to come.

III

Up to now we have been dealing with the first two of our country's three commitments in the area of religion, its commitment to religious pluralism and its commitment to religious freedom. I wish now to speak of the third, which is our traditional belief in the importance of religious witness. The key issue is, of course, what kind of religious witness do we as a people think important. The dilemma faced by the churches will be clear, I think, if we reflect for a moment on the fact that structures of society always have a profound effect upon one's religious consciousness. This is, indeed, the basic insight of sociology: whenever public institutions change in any way, they inevitably affect a people's awareness of themselves, their values and their ideas. Hence every expression of religious witness is destined to some extent to bear the marks of the society in which it is produced. This does not mean that such witness is totally relativized by society, but only that its expression is always relational, that is to say, its norm of truth and error is always exercised within a social context and under the influence of a particular social ethos.[27] I noted already what has perhaps been the most important public influence upon religious witness in America, namely, the conviction by the Founders that what the churches held in common, "the essentials of every religion," was vital for the health of the nation, but not what they held separately as particular tenets of their own faith. This early conviction has been from time to time the source of no little confusion among the churches as to what their primary religious witness should be in a pluralistic land. Let us look at the situation more closely.

I think it safe to say that genuine religious witness, combining authentic faith with contemporary relevance, is a rare thing. Institutional religion usually suffers from one of two types of irrelevance: either it retains meaning for its members on the personal level but loses it for a society at large, or it manages to be historically relevant in the public realm but of little or no significance for the needs of ordinary people. The United States knows this dilemma well: the Protestant, Catholic, and Jewish religions have tended historically either to give a witness that, though genuinely cultural, raises no disturbing religious questions on the personal level, or to give one that is truly prophetic and relevant to the needs of persons, but that spiritually isolates them from dominant cultural trends. This is because the American value system has always been a mixture of the secular and sacred, as I have tried to show, and American religion has generally exhibited the same sort of value mix. Churches and synagogues were able to cope so easily with the secularization of the twentieth century because to a certain extent they had incorporated many of society's secular values into their own systems of thought and bureaucratic structures, thereby exposing themselves to the dilemma of religious witness I just mentioned. Religion was given a very specific role as a Sunday affair. To mention it on weekdays meant that one was expected to speak in terms of a morality acceptable to the nation as a whole, or not speak at all.

Hence the fundamental problem to be faced today: granted that the structures of society always affect religious consciousness, what must be the corresponding influence of the religious mind upon society? Surely the role of religion cannot be to go on legitimizing the social and political *status quo,* or to continue confirming our country in its mediocrity and self-satisfaction. My own answer to this problem is simply to underscore and italicize the perennial response of the thoughtful citizen: religion in America must return to its historic vocation as judge of society; it must activate anew its traditional prophetic witness to mystery and justice in the world. It is the flattening out of life to the totally understandable and the fully controlled which is the great inhibitor of human freedom. And it is the injustice and petty tyrannies in society which, if left unchallenged, distort God's image in the individual and dull the public's moral sensitivity to evil.

Religious truth as critique of society must begin, then, with a call to the nation to recognize the ultimate mystery which surrounds all things human. This transcendental dimension in the lives of individuals and peoples can never be collapsed by the certainties of science or philosophy. To believe that it could would be to assert that human fear and self-doubt are rooted outside the person, and that the only thing needed to correct the malfunctioning of society is some bureaucratic solution to problems of hunger, population, ecology, and war. Such an outlook inevitably leads to a kind of exaggerated rationalism, whereby we become too sure of our national purpose to tolerate dissent, too uncritical of our limitations to be saved from self-righteousness and pride. Technologies and ideologies, necessary though they are for any national ethos, always originate from a mix of good and evil, for all human virtue is mixed with some element of ambiguity. Society in other words must always use imperfect tools, and religion's role is to submit these tools to judgment, relativizing them, putting them in their place, reminding a nation that human perversity is a reality and that a people who do not count on its presence are both sinners and fools.[28]

This witness to mystery and transcendence is not easy to concretize or specify. It is not the task of church or synagogue to provide a basis for political decisions so much as to create an atmosphere within which these can be wisely made, to shape certain patterns of national thinking which can then act as a check upon elements in society which tend to damage the humanity of its members. One theologian, Edward Schillebeeckx, has characterized this approach as one of "critical negativity," by which he means a positive power exercising constant pressure to bring about what is most desirable for society, not by any explicit formulation but by negative knowledge.[29] Hence believers have as little positive idea as nonbelievers of what is worthy of the person. They too have to seek fumblingly and consider various alternatives, keeping in mind, as they search, human values already realized in history. If they protest certain public situations or goals, they do so in the name of personal values still being sought and revealed negatively, in the contrast-experience of what is unworthy of human dignity. Thus in recent years religious leaders have publicly criticized racial inequality, thereby giving religious legitimation to the civil rights movement. With somewhat less unanimity they also protested our involvement in Vietnam, thereby withdrawing such legitimation from a policy judged to be violative of the rights and dignity of the Indo-

chinese. Ideally this critical function of religion ought
to be directed at everything that prevents men and
women from transcending their limitations, against every skepticism of the human potential, against every
effort to consider persons as either matter or means for
constructing some rationalized technological future.

But if prophetic witness to mystery is not to be shal-
low, it must be accompanied by an equally strong witness to justice as a moral imperative. The reason is that
the central Judeo-Christian message of love of God and
love of neighbor is radically incompatible with the unjust treatment of another human being. How can you
love someone and treat him unjustly? Just as we are
never sure we love God unless we love our fellow human beings, so we are never sure that we love at all
unless our love is sensitive to the demands of justice.
This clear religious imperative, however, has become
extremely complex and enormously difficult to carry
out because in our time injustice has come to be seen
not only as an individual but as a social phenomenon:
millions of men and women are hungry, diseased, and
abjectly poor not because they are lazy and will not
work, but because social structures and systems of
power make them so by an unfair distribution of human
resources and wealth. Vast numbers in the Third World
now experience what has been called "institutionalized
violence," by which is meant an economic and social
order so organized in favor of the privileged classes that
the masses are forced to live in an inhuman condition.
Between 5 and 10 percent of the population of Latin
America now control over half its wealth; half the people on our planet have a per capita income of $100 a
year; a third of the world suffers from malnutrition and
half a million die of starvation annually; more money is
spent each year on the average American dog than on
the average child in a poor country of Latin America,

114   *Religion and the American Dream*

Asia, or Africa.[30] The poor of the undeveloped countries now know all this and know, too, that it need not be so. All these gross social inequities can be corrected, but it is becoming increasingly clear that, despite the opportunities offered by an ever more serviceable technology, men and women in the developed countries are simply not willing to pay the price of a more just and humane social order.

It does not follow from this grim picture of societal injustice that churches ought to think of themselves as agents for curing social ills. They are neither more nor less than witnesses to a moral imperative. Nor do I wish to imply that changes in social structures can of themselves satisfy religious needs—although we should remember the words of Gandhi: "To the hungry man God does not dare to appear except in the form of bread." What I am saying is simply that there are some social situations where churches alone have enough independence and courage to denounce injustice. They ought not spend all their time echoing secular clichés, but they also ought never be afraid of reinforcing a contemporary trend. The cause of the Third World does not become less important because it is fashionable. A church or synagogue that rouses its members from lethargy and sensitizes them to the social dimensions of their faith does not become thereby a welfare agency or a spiritual Red Cross. The role of religious leaders in this decisive area is precisely the formation of a community with a conscience, one that does not withhold compassion by pleading complexity. Such a community will recognize that, because we are all brothers and sisters to everyone else, we all stand under a common judgment. "Will we ever achieve justice in Athens?" The wise Greek who was asked this question replied: "We will achieve justice when those who are not injured are as indignant as those who are." This outlook stands in stark contrast with a recent survey in which Americans ranked economic aid and loans to the poor no higher than 20th on a list of 23 areas in which they would like to see their tax money spent.[31]

This last item highlights the point where the chief emphasis in the area of justice must fall today. Americans are hampered in responding to the need for massive social action on a world scale because of our country's all-pervasive emphasis on private rights and interests. National well-being has come to be identified with a very individualistic understanding of the pursuit of happiness, quite unlike that of the Founders. As a result most Americans today are not very much interested in the common good of the larger world community, some even insisting that the promise of a better life be fulfilled at home first, no matter what the international consequences. This is a peculiarly American form of blindness, and because it is rooted in societal reality it can be healed only by some societal change. Eventually government will have to act to ensure more equal access to economic wealth and cultural resources. But in the meantime the people of our country must be sensitized to what their religions say about committing oneself to institutions serving the needs of a more and more integrated human family.[32] The great resource here is the original Judeo-Christian tradition which placed the community at the center of the people's awareness and presented individual life as a participation in the larger life of the community. Religious leaders in America must ask themselves to what extent they have appropriated this original tradition. To what extent have they allowed it to correct their inherited perception of society conditioned by the American preoccupation with private rights and interest? For them to attempt a prophetic witness to justice without such a corrected perception would be as ineffective as

the game described by Gilbert and Sullivan's Mikado
"on a cloth untrue with a twisted cue and elliptical
billiard balls."

IV

Before we conclude our treatment of America's
threefold religious belief, let me make one observation
and urge one very serious caution. The observation is
this: the importance of religion in a democracy is that
it provides a ground above and beyond the political
upon which to base a sense of personal dignity and the
claim to personal freedom. Most Americans are convinced that individual destiny transcends that of the
body politic because they believe in the personal God
of the Bible, who guides each human being by his Providence within one of the communities of the Judeo-
Christian heritage. Without such religious roots it is not
at all clear that belief in responsible self-government
could be maintained; for political freedom does not
finally depend upon restrictive measures and legal
sanctions but upon each citizen's recognizing his duty
to the republic. Religion gives him the motives and
norms for doing this duty, for using his freedom to
follow moral imperatives and not to pursue criminal
goals. The concept of limited government originated
precisely in this notion that there is an Authority above
the authority of the state and a transcendent moral law
binding on all persons.[33] I therefore interpret the religion clauses of the First Amendment as a formal manifestation of concern that religion flourish in the nation,
through a guarantee of its pluralism, of its freedom
from all government interference, and of the importance of its public witness.

I urge one caution, however, and it concerns the
mode of bearing religious witness. Religious leaders

must inevitably assert moral standards in speaking out on public issues. It is in this way that they summon the nation to live up to its own ideals and to value those courses of action which benefit the whole of society. All of this is good and necessary for the people's welfare. But there is the perennial danger that a given religious community will transfer the authority it exercises over its own members to the larger human community, and seek to change the beliefs of others not by persuasion but by one or another form of coercion. Hence it is extremely important to distinguish between what is regarded as morally evil by one or another church body and what ought to be made a civil crime, between what one regards as right for oneself and what one insists should be imposed by law upon all. This is not to say that laws may not impose moral and religious values. Civil rights legislation obviously does. But here there is a clear national consensus against discrimination and in favor of equal opportunity for all citizens regardless of sex or race. Disagreements center, not upon the moral value in question, but upon such means as busing or employment laws enacted to institutionalize the moral value.

The problem arises, therefore, when there is no clear national consensus on some moral question and none can be created by persuasion. What is to be done then? For the religious pluralism established by the First Amendment has meant historically that the country is, more often than not, morally pluralistic on most matters. I think that in general the paradigm ought to be the way church bodies behave toward each other. One church may regard the beliefs of another as intolerable, but they both manage to live together peacefully. They do not picket each other, though there would be nothing illegal in their doing so. Church bodies ought to deal with society at large in the same way. They need to know not what is legally admissible but what is politically and spiritually prudent. If they do not find a national consensus for their moral position, then they ought not use political or economic pressure to prohibit by law what large numbers believe to be morally good. Everyone acknowledges today that the Eighteenth Amendment, prohibiting the sale of intoxicating liquors, was disastrous. Many fear that some amendments now being advocated to prohibit abortion would be equally disastrous, and for the same reasons.[34]

In the case of abortion, of course, a crucial element alters the paradigm: the beliefs of one church are rarely perceived by another as inherently harmful and unjust to innocent third parties, whereas abortion is perceived by many as the taking of human life and the radical denial of rights to the fetus. Hence we have here a much more complex situation, especially since many others in our society experience a compelling moral obligation to alleviate situations that are oppressive and harmful to women. These two opposing groups find it impossible to coexist peacefully; their contradictory moral imperatives make public conflict inevitable. But once again, because no national consensus exists, the conflict ought to remain in the public forum. Each side must be enabled to make its moral appeal to the other openly and vigorously. Law should be used to mediate the conflict, not wielded like a bludgeon to resolve it prematurely. Decisions of the judicial process must be tolerated even when they are not accepted. Even in the case of abortion religious people must finally "suffer the cultural propagation of what they regard as an 'error'—not because of an indifference to what they hold to be true but because the free society as a whole, unlike its individual members, must treat cultural 'truths,' even the most staunchly held, *as if* they were tentative."[35] The witness of church leaders must indeed be outspoken and courageous, but it should remain a religious witness and not allow itself to be transformed into a political lobby. In matters religious, long-term conversion of heart is always to be preferred to stonewalling.

CONCLUSION

The reader may well believe that these chapters have opened up more problems than they have resolved. One such unresolved problem overarches all the rest, in my opinion, and by way of conclusion I would like to relate it to some of the major themes I have been developing. Briefly stated it is this: Will the American tradition of human rights succeed in expanding its original individualized and highly defensive framework into one that can affirm rights for humankind which are positive, comprehensive, communal, and social? I believe that whether we hope or despair for the American dream hinges upon whether we adequately negotiate this formidable passage.

This is so fundamental a question because it accurately mirrors the profound change that has taken place in both the human community and the human psyche since the United States came into being as a nation. Two hundred years ago everyone believed that the human race was destined to develop as a multiplicity of individuals, each achieving maximum growth more or less in isolation, protected from government and from each other by suitable guarantees of freedom and autonomy. Today, as we noted in Chapters 1 and 2, nothing is clearer than the fact that we are all involved in a socializing process of planetary proportions, which is moving irresistibly toward some form of psychic solidarity for the human family. All our great problems are now global: overpopulation, environmental collapse, depletion of natural resources, and the specter of a nuclear holocaust. A new world view is being forced upon us, one that no longer accepts family, neighborhood, and nation as our only centers of concern, with the rest of the human race somehow distanced and outside. Our problem is not so much to recognize this collective consciousness, since it is so obvious, as to harmonize it with values traditionally associated with the individualized personality. An assertion of human rights can no longer simply aim at the highest degree of independence for the individual in society. Rather it must seek, as Pierre Teilhard de Chardin urged almost thirty years ago in UNESCO, to define the conditions under which the slow collectivization of the species can be accomplished without impairing that singularity of being which each of us possesses. "We must no longer seek to organize the world in favor of, and in terms of, the isolated individual; we must try to combine all things for the perfection ('personalization') of the individual by his well-ordered integration with the unified group."[1]

Now the human rights tradition of the Founders, which has been the foundation of our country's whole cultural development, can adapt to this outlook only with great difficulty. Alfred North Whitehead believed that behind even the most abstract philosophical system there was a hidden imaginative background. Behind the Bill of Rights, those first ten amendments to the Constitution, was the image of an endless frontier on an endless continent. Religious pluralism, as we saw, was in no small measure influenced by this image. Social cooperation was everywhere taken for granted as a necessity of life in America. There was no need for government to foster such communal consciousness. Hence the sole task of the legal structure which was finally embodied in the Constitution was to dispense power and to circumscribe government intervention. This was further specified in the first set of amendments, all of which involve procedures for implementing the basic rights of individual self-determination. "The Bill of Rights explicitly guarantees rights which are defensive. . . . They do not enable [persons] to accomplish definable purposes. Virtually the only source of threat was governmental incursion. The rights which became legal ones, then, specified limitations on those types of activity which the government might undertake to curtail self-determination."[2] Hence any governmental action to establish religion or abridge freedom of speech, press, assembly, and petition is specifically proscribed. There were to be no unreasonable searches and seizures, no cruel and unusual punishment, and due process was to be observed in all criminal prosecution and before the taking of life, liberty, or property.

However, built into the Constitution was a system of revision, involving further amendment and judicial review, which allowed for a specification of other rights. The obvious ones were those which eventually extended and clarified the essentially protective rights originally specified, in the way that freedom of the press was extended over against libel law. But another class of rights was gradually articulated also, one aimed at guaranteeing such goods and services as were necessary to achieve sufficient material status to sustain self-determination. These did not fare so well over the years, however, because they depended upon a normative definition of human dignity and the human person, something the Founders did not think necessary to provide. The legalization of such social rights has thus been avoided whenever possible, because such legalization would be a demand upon specified persons to fulfill certain duties toward others; and without a normative definition of personal dignity there could be no specification of duties corresponding to rights. Indeed, "this concept of duty is foreign to the American constitutional framework. While contracts may bind, no person or group has a duty of any sort, except to government. This holds even when the agent in question has the capacity to render the service required by another's right."[3] Only in the area of education has the legalization of this second class of rights been to some extent successful, because the Due Process and Equal Protection Clauses of the Fourteenth Amendment have been used by the courts to force this question at the procedural level. But these rights never leave this level; they remain rights to certain proper procedures and are rarely if ever allowed to reach the more substantive question of duties.

A good example of this anomaly on the legislative level is the debate in Congress on the "right to health care."[4] Many are puzzled at the whole concept of such a "right," since it has been taken for granted until very recently that health care was a privilege. To call it a "right" means that there must also be a duty on the part of specified agents to secure that right. Unlike the negative promotion required by rights like freedom of expression (achieved simply by noninterference), the right to health care, if it is affirmed for all citizens, demands very positive promotion, a social cooperation of a very high degree on the part of multiple agencies in the nation. This means the need for legislation that will equitably distribute the economic burden of health care through the whole of society, rather than impose it upon a few agencies (such as the medical profession and private insurance companies). Hence the further need for some persuasive grounding of the right as an extension of the original rights tradition of the Founders. Their concept of "public happiness," discussed in Chapter 2, could well provide such a grounding. Such public happiness cannot be pursued if there is an obvious and unjustifiable disparity between the health care available to some citizens and that available to others, when in fact we are capable as a society of providing adequate care for all. It is no accident, however, that this pursuit of public happiness as an unalienable right has become clouded in the American psyche. Deep in that psyche is the conviction that the idea of the good is essentially private, not public and common.

This conviction has been brilliantly argued in a recent study by Harvard's Robert Nozick, *Anarchy, State and Utopia,* winner of a National Book Award for 1975 and object of avid interest from policymakers in Washington. There is no such thing as an overall social good, insists Nozick, "no *social entity* with a good that undergoes some sacrifice for its own good. There are only individual people, different individual people, with their own individual lives. Using one of these people for the benefit of others, uses him and benefits the others. Nothing more."[5] All theories of distributive justice thus lose their foundation, and the state is required to do only what is minimally necessary to protect the individual citizen and his property. There is, of course, no lack of scholarly writings that argue exactly the opposite, as does John Rawls's *A Theory of Justice,*[6] but Nozick represents the thinking of that solid segment of the nation which has always seen egalitarian policies as infringements upon economic and political freedom. Like the right of all to health care, however, such policies are necessary before another segment of the nation, namely, the poor, can have any experience at all of the freedom already possessed by the upper and middle classes. It is usually the poor who have civil liberties violated and due process denied. A minimal state could mean that they would starve or die in a recession, because there was no welfare program to give them food stamps or to supply them with medicine. The poor, in other words, simply cannot afford freedom from government interference. Increasing the power of the state by appropriate social legislation may thus be the only way to link the pursuit of public happiness for all persons with their psychological and physical well-being in society.

This struggle between the individualistic tradition that dominated our past and the present emerging collective consciousness can likewise be seen on the judicial level in America. It is generally agreed today that a broad egalitarianism was the chief characteristic of Supreme Court decisions during the 1950's and 1960's. That was most evident in racial issues and in decisions leveling qualifications for voting, but it was strong also in procedural decisions aimed at minimizing the disadvantages of the poor.[7] In landmark decisions like the 1954 *Brown* v. *Board of Education,* which declared racial segregation unconstitutional, the Court drew the attention of the country to issues of the highest principle which had gone unheeded for decades. No longer was the Court the conservative force of former times, acting to restrict liberal Congresses, Presidents, and state governments. Under Chief Justice Earl Warren a very different type of judiciary begins to emerge, which does not hesitate to confront more conservative executives and legislatures. This is why the classic insight of Max Lerner in 1937 now has to be modified: the nine Justices may still be viewed by the nation as nine high priests interpreting the sacred text of the Constitution,[8] but their interpretations are no longer necessarily viewed as either definitive or sacrosanct. Those for whom the individual and the individual's interest and welfare are the sole test of a good society are especially afraid that we are gradually moving toward arbitrary rule by unreachable authorities, a kind of "krytocracy," to use Justice Stanley F. Reed's term, a "government by judges."[9]

Nevertheless, judicial concern for the communal and social rights of citizens continues, the Court quietly testing the people's hopes for the present social order. We have discussed at some length the Court's concern for freedom of expression in our society. With this and other concerns it "has occasionally pushed beyond established constitutional contours to protect the vulnerable and to further basic human values."[10] This observation of Justice Thurgood Marshall is admirably illustrated by the expansion of the law of privacy in the mid-sixties. Originally a device in the law of torts to protect the few from the curiosity of the many (usually intrusion from newspapers and prying neighbors), it has gradually been developed into a principle of constitutional law aimed at limiting the power of government to intrude at all into certain areas of human activity. Ultimately the reason for this development is that the original basis for judicial recognition of a right to privacy was the principle of "inviolate personality" elaborated in a famous 1890 article in the *Harvard Law Review*.[11] Such a principle, however, could hardly be kept as the preserve of the few. In 1968, for example, it became the basis of Justice Potter Stewart's position, in *Katz* v. *U.S.*, that the Fourth Amendment protects people, not places: even in an area accessible to the public, what a person seeks to preserve as private may be constitutionally protected against invasion by electronic eavesdropping.[12] During the same period the right of privacy was held to extend to activities relating to marriage, procreation, and family relationships, and to provide a refuge from data banks, credit checks, and government surveillance of what one reads in one's home. The egalitarian sweep of all these decisions is clearly an attempt to elaborate, through judicial review, a more comprehensive set of human rights (as distinguished from property rights) than that provided by the rights tradition of the Founders. Through its judiciary the country is thus groping slowly toward some normative understanding of human dignity, which it must have before it can successfully grapple with the larger questions of human existence posed today by the global community.

"The designer of a culture is not an interloper or a meddler," says B. F. Skinner. "He does not step in to disturb a natural process, he is part of a natural process. The geneticist who changes the characteristics of a species by selective breeding or by changing genes may seem to be meddling in biological evolution, but he does so because his species has evolved to the point at which it has been able to develop a science of genetics and a culture which induces its members to take the future of the species into account."[13] What Skinner sees taking place in genetics today is trying to take place also in American constitutional theory. On the legislative and judicial levels our human rights tradition is gradually being modified. Whether such modification will enable it to affirm more positive and communal rights for humankind is still to be seen. As a people we continue to support economic and social racism at home as well as oppressive governments abroad. We say that our values come from a conviction of what it means to be human in civil society. But does our commitment to the religion clauses of the First Amendment really make us want to promote the rights of conscience around the world? The Judeo-Christian tradition insists that God's designs can never simply be identified with

those of one's country at a given time. The religion of
the republic will incorporate this realization only if we
are aware that our constitutional heritage has to be
continually reexamined, broadened, and brought into
harmony with the larger communal aspirations of the
human spirit.

I have talked at sufficient length in these chapters
about the "shadow" of our corporate psyche, to use
Carl Jung's suggestive term. But knowledge of this
"shadow" is not something merely negative. Through
self-knowledge we come to terms with our instincts as
a nation, and this should throw some light on those
powers slumbering in our psyche which would elude us
were everything to go well. "They are potentialities of
the greatest dynamism," says Jung, "and it depends
entirely on the preparedness and attitude of the conscious mind whether the irruption of these forces and
the images and ideas associated with them will tend
toward construction or catastrophe."[14] We know now
that the American Revolution was so successful because
it was one-sided. It was made by a small population with
enormous resources, true political freedom, and the
experience of representative government. The Founders could therefore create a new and independent political system, but there was no need for them to create
a new society.[15] Thus their achievement has not really
helped us to understand the great social revolutions of
our present century, which have had to be made
against desperate poverty and massive inequality. This
is surely one reason we have been so slow to overcome
the racial injustice that has characterized our society
for two centuries. Yet the fact is that we *are* coming
slowly to understand social revolution, and we *are* coming to grips with racial injustice in our land. These are
indications that we *are* negotiating some transition to
that outlook on life in civil society which is coming to

characterize the species as a whole. How we judge the success or failure of these changes and transitions will largely determine whether we hope or despair for the success of the American dream.

NOTES

INTRODUCTION

1. Edmund Burke, *Reflections on the Revolution in France* (The Bobbs-Merrill Company, Inc., 1955), pp. 288–289.

2. See the perceptive treatment of this dilemma by Robert Bosc, "Questions for the American People," *America*, Nov. 22, 1975, pp. 355–357.

Chapter 1
A NEW ORDER FOR THE AGES

1. Daniel J. Boorstin, *The Americans* (Random House, Inc., 1958), p. 19. See the interpretation of this material given by Hannah Arendt, *On Revolution* (The Viking Press, Inc., 1965), pp. 212–213.

2. Seymour Martin Lipset, *The First New Nation* (Basic Books, Inc., 1963), develops this theme at great length.

3. John Adams, quoted by Hannah Arendt, *op. cit.*, p. 15.

4. Romans 5:20. See the perceptive treatment of this subject by Thomas E. Clarke, "Societal Grace," in *Soundings* (Washington, D.C.: Center of Concern, 1974), pp. 15–17. That this question is still very much alive and controversial is evident from the *Hartford Appeal for Theological Affirmation* issued in January 1975 by religious thinkers from nine Christian denominations. For the text of the *Appeal*, see the

April 1975 issue of *Worldview,* as well as the subsequent symposium in the issues for May and June 1975.

5. Alexis de Tocqueville, *Democracy in America* (Vintage Books, Inc., 1954), Vol. I, p. 314.

6. Gilbert K. Chesterton, *What I Saw in America* (Dodd, Mead & Company, Inc., 1922), pp. 11–12, 7.

7. Saul K. Padover (ed.), *The Complete Jefferson* (Duell, Sloan & Pearce, Inc., 1943), p. 414.

8. Saxe Commins (ed.), *Basic Writings of George Washington* (Random House, Inc., 1948), p. 559.

9. Max Lerner, *America as a Civilization* (Simon & Schuster, Inc., 1957), p. 715.

10. Hannah Arendt (*op. cit.,* p. 205) has pointed out the importance of such remembering for the American psyche. The covenant theme in the colonial experience has been developed and documented by many authors, most recently by Robert N. Bellah, *The Broken Covenant* (The Seabury Press, Inc., 1975).

11. Philip Van Doren Stern (ed.), *The Life and Writings of Abraham Lincoln* (Modern Library, Inc., 1940), pp. 841–842, 788. See Robert N. Bellah, "Civil Religion in America," in Russell E. Richey and Donald G. Jones (eds.), *American Civil Religion* (Harper & Row, Publishers, Inc., 1974), pp. 31–33. Bellah's celebrated article was originally published in the Winter 1967 issue of *Daedalus,* the Journal of the American Academy of Arts and Sciences.

12. *Dred Scott* v. *Sandford,* 19 How. 393, 404 (1857).

13. In an address to the New Jersey Senate in February 1961. Cited in William J. Wolf, *The Almost Chosen People: A Study of the Religion of Abraham Lincoln* (Pilgrim Press, 1970), p. 13. I have found very thoughtful discussion of this ambiguity in the American vision in Robert Benne and Philip Hefner, *Defining America* (Fortress Press, 1974), pp. 99–111.

14. Sydney E. Ahlstrom has given a remarkable overview of the origins and shortcomings of American ideals: "The American National Faith: Humane, Yet All Too Human," in *The Changing Nature of America's Civil Religion,* papers given originally at the Aspen Institute for Humanistic Studies and subsequently published by the Institute in June 1973.

W. Lloyd Warner has described the Memorial Day service at length in "An American Sacred Ceremony," in Richey and Jones (eds.), *op. cit.,* pp. 89–111.

15. Sidney E. Mead, *The Lively Experiment: The Shaping of Christianity in America* (Harper & Row, Publishers, Inc., 1963), p. 75.

16. Albert J. Beveridge, quoted in Ernest Lee Tuveson, *Redeemer Nation: The Idea of America's Millennial Role* (The University of Chicago Press, 1968), p. vii.

17. Will Herberg, *Protestant—Catholic—Jew* (Doubleday & Company, Inc., Anchor Books, 1960), p. 268.

18. Charles P. Henderson, Jr., *The Nixon Theology* (Harper & Row, Publishers, Inc., 1972), p. 193.

19. In formulating this position, I have expressed the opinions of different people: Martin E. Marty, "A Nation of Behavers," *Worldview,* May 1974, pp. 9–13; Leo Pfeffer, "Commentary on *Civil Religion in America,*" in Donald R. Cutler (ed.), *The Religious Situation, 1968* (Beacon Press, Inc., 1968), pp. 360–365; Sidney E. Mead, "In Quest of America's Religion," *The Christian Century,* June 17, 1970, pp. 752–756.

20. Cf. Bellah, "Civil Religion," in Richey and Jones (eds.), *op. cit.,* pp. 33–36; Sidney E. Mead, "The Nation with the Soul of a Church," in *ibid.,* p. 60. This confrontation has been well described by Marty, *loc. cit.,* and by Conrad Cherry, *God's New Israel: Religious Interpretation of American Destiny* (Prentice-Hall, Inc., 1971), pp. 15–20.

21. See Bellah's "Response" in Cutler (ed.), *op. cit.,* pp. 388–392.

22. Mead, "The Nation," in Richey and Jones (eds.), *op. cit.,* p. 60.

23. Sydney E. Ahlstrom, *A Religious History of the American People* (Yale University Press, 1973), pp. 1080–1081.

24. Benne and Hefner, *op. cit.,* p. vii.

25. Lerner, *op. cit.,* pp. 948–949.

26. William Fulbright, quoted in *The New York Times,* Nov. 4, 1974.

27. Benne and Hefner, *op. cit.,* p. 116.

28. See on this question Cherry, *op. cit.,* pp. 19–20; Robert

N. Bellah, "Evil and the American Ethos," in Nevitt Sanford and Craig Comstock (eds.), *Sanctions for Evil* (Jossey-Bass, Inc., Publishers, 1971), p. 187.

29. Benne and Hefner, *op. cit.,* p. 101. I have followed here their development of this topic.

30. William Lee Miller, *Of Thee, Nevertheless, I Sing* (Harcourt Brace Jovanovich, Inc., 1975).

Chapter 2
The Pursuit of Happiness

1. Robert Bellah uses this method in his treatment of tradition in *The Broken Covenant.*

2. Arendt, *On Revolution,* p. 237.

3. From an unpublished paper of Paul Ricoeur delivered in 1971 at the University of Chicago, quoted by Andrew M. Greeley, "The Civil Religion of Ethnic Americans," *Religious Education,* Vol. LXX (1975), pp. 500–501.

4. Letter of May 8, 1825, to Richard Henry Lee, quoted in Clinton Rossiter, *The Political Thought of the American Revolution* (Harcourt, Brace and World, Inc., 1963), pp. 64–65.

5. Arendt, *op. cit.,* p. 127.

6. Julian P. Boyd, *The Declaration of Independence* (Princeton University Press, 1945), p. 22.

7. I am indebted here to the unpublished manuscript of Francis J. Grogan, "The American Tradition of Revolutionary Liberty," Vol. III, pp. 10ff.

8. Howard Mumford Jones, *The Pursuit of Happiness* (Harvard University Press, 1953), p. 1.

9. Jean Jacques Burlamaqui's *Principles of Natural and Politic Law,* widely read at the time, seems to have been the major source for the conviction that happiness was a right of man and an object of government. The idea, as Grogan's work demonstrates, possesses a whole ancestry that stretches back through the English and continental Middle Ages to the *felicitas aeterna* and *felicitas temporalis* of St. Augustine. William Blackstone's *Commentaries on the Laws of England,* very popular in the colonies, also deals with happiness as an aim of society, and the concept was incorporated in early

1776 into the Virginia Declaration of Rights by George Mason, a close friend of Jefferson's. See Rossiter, *Political Thought*, pp. 59–60, 70–71; also Jones, *op. cit.*, pp. 9–20, 96–97.

10. Rossiter, *Political Thought*, p. 165; Grogan, *loc. cit.*, p. 787. Both authors emphasize the fact that the entire range of Revolutionary literature shows John Locke, the great defender of property, to have been nowhere near the important figure hitherto supposed. "There is no evidence that his treatise . . . sold any better than a half-dozen other books that said much the same thing, and until 1774 his name was mentioned only rarely in the columns of even the most radical newspapers." (Rossiter, *Political Thought*, p. 69.) Locke's subsequent fame as the philosopher of the English Revolution of 1688 is what seems to have made him the one selected by so many American historians as the chief source of ideas for the American Revolution.

11. Padover (ed.), *Complete Jefferson*, p. 6. Hannah Arendt (*op. cit.*, pp. 123ff.) develops these ideas at some length.

12. Joseph Warren's statement, quoted in Rossiter, *Political Thought*, p. 181.

13. Clinton Rossiter, *The First American Revolution* (Harcourt, Brace and World, Inc., 1956), pp. 229–230.

14. James Iredell, quoted by Rossiter, *Political Thought*, p. 113.

15. *Time*, July 14, 1975, p. 19.

16. *Newsweek*, July 28, 1975, p. 72.

17. De Tocqueville, *Democracy in America*, p. 26.

18. Letters of July 12, 1816, and November 13, 1787, quoted by Arendt, *op. cit.*, pp. 235–236.

19. See Bellah, *Broken Covenant*, pp. 32–35 and 142–144, for a further development of this internal aspect of the Revolution.

20. Hannah Arendt makes this point in contrasting the American and French revolutions (*op. cit.*, pp. 219–220).

21. Henry Kissinger, quoted in *The New York Times*, Jan. 4, 1975.

22. For an eloquent statement of the interrelationship be-

tween faith, truth, and the democratic process, see Mead, *Lively Experiment,* pp. 81–87.

23. Jones, *op. cit.,* p. 17.

24. Karl Jaspers, *The Future of Mankind* (The University of Chicago Press, 1961), p. 101.

25. Gunnar Myrdal, quoted by William Lee Miller, *Of Thee, Nevertheless, I Sing,* p. 319.

26. "America's Third Century," a special survey in *The Economist,* Oct. 25, 1975.

27. Pierre Teilhard de Chardin, *Activation of Energy* (Harcourt Brace Jovanovich, Inc., 1971), p. 370.

28. Robert L. Heilbroner, *An Inquiry Into the Human Prospect* (W. W. Norton & Company, Inc., 1974), pp. 114–115, 143–144.

29. Teilhard de Chardin, *Activation of Energy,* p. 231; Pierre Teilhard de Chardin, *The Appearance of Man* (Harper & Row, Publishers, Inc., 1965), p. 169.

30. *Public Papers of the Presidents of the United States,* John F. Kennedy, 1961 (Washington, D.C.: Government Printing Office, 1962), p. 3.

Chapter 3
FREEDOM TO SPEAK

1. Louis D. Brandeis, quoted by Alexander M. Bickel, *The Least Dangerous Branch* (The Bobbs-Merrill Company, Inc., 1962), p. 197.

2. *Ibid.,* p. 25.

3. Eugene V. Rostow, "The Democratic Character of Judicial Review," 66 *Harvard Law Review,* 195 (1952), quoted by Bickel, *Least Dangerous Branch,* p. 26.

4. Charles E. Hughes, quoted in Alexander Meiklejohn, *Free Speech and Its Relation to Self-Government* (Harper & Brothers, 1948), p. 32.

5. *West Virginia Board of Education* v. *Barnette,* 319 U.S. 624, 642 (1943), Justice Robert H. Jackson, speaking for the Court.

6. *Palko* v. *Connecticut,* 302, U.S. 319, 327 (1937), Justice Benjamin N. Cardozo, speaking for the Court.

7. Alexander Meiklejohn, "The First Amendment Is an Absolute," 1961 *The Supreme Court Law Review*, 264 (1961).

8. *Abrams* v. *United States*, 250 U.S. 616, 630 (1919).

9. *United States* v. *Associated Press*, 52 F. Supp. 362, 372 (S.D.N.Y. 1943).

10. *Whitney* v. *California*, 274 U.S. 357, 375–376 (1927).

11. *New York Times* v. *Sullivan*, 376 U.S. 254, 270 (1964); *Associated Press* v. *United States*, 326 U.S. 1, 20 (1945).

12. *Columbia Broadcasting System, Inc.*, v. *Democratic National Committee,* 412 U.S. 94, 189, 191 (1972). (Dissenting opinion.)

13. Padover (ed.), *Complete Jefferson,* pp. 385, 947.

14. Meiklejohn, *Free Speech,* p. 27.

15. Alexander M. Bickel, *The Morality of Consent* (Yale University Press, 1975), pp. 70–72.

16. Thomas I. Emerson, *Toward a General Theory of the First Amendment* (Random House, Inc., Vintage Books, 1967), and *The System of Freedom of Expression* (Random House, Inc., Vintage Books, 1971).

17. Alexander Meiklejohn is the chief proponent of this theory. See *supra*, notes 4 and 7. See also Bickel, *Morality of Consent,* p. 62, and Harry H. Wellington, "Common Law Rules and Constitutional Double Standards: Some Notes on Adjudication," 83 *The Yale Law Review*, 266–270 (1973).

18. Emerson, *System,* p. 7.

19. Learned Hand, quoted by Emerson, *Toward a General Theory,* p. 26.

20. Bickel, *Morality of Consent,* p. 78.

21. *Hudson County Water Co.* v. *McCarter*, 209 U.S. 349, 355 (1908).

22. *Chaplinsky* v. *New Hampshire*, 315 U.S. 568, 571–572 (1942).

23. *Frohwerk* v. *United States*, 249 U.S. 204, 206 (1919).

24. *Schenck* v. *United States*, 249 U.S. 47, 52 (1919).

25. *Beauharnais* v. *Illinois*, 343 U.S. 250, 266 (1952). The last phrase is reference to the principle that where speech otherwise protected by the First Amendment can be shown to present a "clear and present danger" of severe evil which the state has a right to prevent, suppression of that speech

can on occasion be permitted. The principle was elaborated by Justice Holmes in 1919 to deal with the problem of subversive advocacy during World War I. See *Schenck* v. *United States,* 249 U.S. at 52.

26. *Konigsberg* v. *State Bar of California,* 366 U.S. 49n10 (1961).

27. Benjamin N. Cardozo, *The Nature of the Judicial Process* (Yale University Press, 1921), p. 51.

28. Harry Kalven, Jr., "The New York Times Case: A Note on 'The Central Meaning of the First Amendment,' " 1964 *The Supreme Court Law Review,* 194 (1964).

29. Emerson, *System,* p. 522. See his analysis of the case and its significance, which I follow here, pp. 520–543.

30. *New York Times* v. *Sullivan,* 376 U.S. at 269, 270, 271.

31. *Ibid.,* at 271–272, 279, 279–280, 285–286.

32. This "central meaning" is discussed in connection with the Court's declaring unconstitutional the Alien and Sedition Act of 1798, *ibid.,* at 273ff. Harry Kalven, Jr. ("The New York Times Case," pp. 204ff.), suggests that the Court's focus on this Act's unconstitutionality is the key to understanding the whole decision. From now on, he says, analysis of free speech issues should "begin with the significant issue of seditious libel and defamation of government by its critics rather than with the sterile example of a man falsely yelling fire in a crowded theater."

33. *Garrison* v. *Louisiana,* 279 U.S. 64, 75 (1964).

34. *Curtis Publishing Co.* v. *Butts,* 388 U.S. 130, 154–155 (1967). "Public figure" is there defined as one who has in general "commanded a substantial amount of independent public interest," or who becomes a public figure by "a thrusting of his personality into the 'vortex' of an important public controversy."

35. *Gertz* v. *Robert Welch, Inc.,* 418 U.S. 323 (1974).

36. In the 1967 privacy case, *Time* v. *Hill,* 385 U.S. 374, the Court applied the actual malice rule to false or fictitious accounts of all "newsworthy" persons. The privacy of such individuals must yield to freedom of the press unless malicious falsehood is involved. See Emerson, *System,* pp. 544–561.

37. See on this point, Kalven, "The New York Times Case," pp. 192–193.

38. *Mills* v. *Alabama,* 384 U.S. 214, 219 (1966).

39. Bickel, *Morality of Consent,* pp. 83–87.

40. Thomas Jefferson, quoted in the concurring opinion of Justice William O. Douglas in *Columbia Broadcasting System, Inc.,* v. *Democratic National Committee,* 412 U.S. at 153.

41. *Miami Herald Publishing Co.* v. *Tornillo,* 418 U.S. 241, 260 (1974).

42. *Ibid.*

43. *New York Times Co.* v. *United States,* 403 U.S. 713 (1971).

44. Meiklejohn, *Free Speech,* p. 88.

45. *Associated Press* v. *United States,* 326 U.S. 1, 20 (1945).

46. Jerome A. Barron, "Access to the Press—A New First Amendment Right," in David G. Clark and Earl R. Hutchison (eds.), *Mass Media and the Law* (Interscience Publishers, Inc., 1970), pp. 421–461. This essay originally appeared in 1967 in *Harvard Law Review.*

47. Emerson, *System,* p. 630. His full treatment of this problem is given on pp. 627–673.

48. *Ibid.,* p. 634.

49. *Olmstead* v. *United States,* 277 U.S. 438, 479 (1928). (Dissenting opinion.)

50. *Beauharnais* v. *Illinois,* 343 U.S. at 274. (Dissenting opinion.)

51. The comparison is that of Emerson, *System,* p. 662. His point is that scarcity is not to be predicated upon a comparison between the number of stations and the number of newspapers in a given area, but on the number of people wishing to broadcast.

52. *National Broadcasting Co.* v. *United States,* 319 U.S. 190, 227, 215–216 (1943).

53. 1959 amendment of the Communications Act, 47 U.S.C. § 315 (a).

54. *Red Lion Broadcasting Co.* v. *FCC,* 395 U.S. 367, 390, 389, 394 (1969). Justice Douglas did not participate in this unanimous decision and said later that "with all respect" he would not support it. See his concurring opinion in *Columbia*

Broadcasting System v. *Democratic National Committee,* 412 U.S. at 155.

55. Emerson, *System,* p. 663.

56. *Red Lion Broadcasting Co.* v. *FCC,* 395 U.S. at 393–394.

57. See the development of broadcasters' complaints and references to sources in Judge Edward A. Tamm's opinion in *Brandywine–Main Line Radio, Inc.,* v. *FCC,* 473 F.2d 16, 77–79 (1972).

58. In "What's Fair on the Air," *The New York Times Magazine,* March 30, 1975, pp. 11ff., Fred W. Friendly has explored efforts of both the Kennedy and Nixon Administrations to exploit the fairness doctrine as a political instrument.

59. The point has been argued with vigor by Jerome A. Barron, "An Emerging First Amendment Right of Access to the Media," 37 *George Washington Law Review,* 503ff. (1969).

60. The issue was well stated by Justice Brennan in his dissenting opinion: "The First Amendment values of individual self-expression and individual participation in public debate are central to our concept of liberty. If these values are to survive in an age of technology, it is essential that individuals be permitted at least *some* opportunity to express their views over the electronic media. Balancing those interests against the limited interest of broadcasters in exercising 'journalistic supervision' over the mere allocation of *advertising* time . . . , I simply cannot conclude that the interest of broadcasters must prevail." *Columbia Broadcasting System* v. *Democratic National Committee,* 412 U.S. at 201.

61. Judge Skelly Wright, speaking for the D.C. Circuit Court of Appeals, held that the First Amendment compels the FCC to require broadcasters to accept *some* advertising of this type, though not necessarily any particular advertisement. His reason was that an *absolute* ban would mean that a private citizen could *never* exercise the initiative by taking editorial control into his own hands on what is essentially a public forum, like a park, a schoolroom, or a town meeting hall; whereas the right to speak can only flourish if it is allowed to operate in some effective forum. See *Business Ex-*

ecutives' Move for Vietnam Peace v. *FCC*, 450 F.2d 642 (1971).

62. *Columbia Broadcasting System* v. *Democratic National Committee*, 412 U.S. at 124–125.

63. *Ibid.*, at 146. (Concurring opinion of Justice Potter Stewart.)

64. Judge David L. Bazelon has so argued in his dissent in *Brandywine–Main Line Radio, Inc.*, v. *FCC*, 473 F.2d at 79.

65. See the treatment of this question by Harry Kalven, Jr., "Broadcasting, Public Policy and the First Amendment," 10 *Journal of Law and Economics*, 15–49 (1967).

66. Studies of the influence of radio and television have multiplied in recent years. The present data is from *An Extended View of Public Attitudes Toward Television and Other Mass Media, 1959–1971*. A Report of the Roper Organization, Inc., 1971.

67. Bellah, *Broken Covenant*, p. 84.

68. Bickel, *Morality of Consent*, pp. 60–61.

69. *Ibid.*, p. 12.

70. See Mead, *Lively Experiment*, pp. 81–86.

71. *Public Papers of the Presidents of the United States*, Lyndon B. Johnson, 1965 (Washington, D.C.: Government Printing Office, 1966), p. 73.

Chapter 4
THE CHURCHES IN A PLURALISTIC LAND

1. Winfred E. Garrison, "Characteristics of American Organized Religion," in *Annals of the American Academy of Political and Social Sciences*, Vol. CCLVI (1948), p. 17, quoted by Mead, *Lively Experiment*, p. 192.

2. This observation has been made by a number of authors; for example, Sidney E. Mead, "The Fact of Pluralism and the Persistence of Sectarianism," in Elwyn A. Smith (ed.), *The Religion of the Republic* (Fortress Press, 1971), pp. 258–259; Loren P. Beth, *The American Theory of Church and State* (University of Florida Press, 1958), pp. 141–142.

3. See Mead, *Lively Experiment*, pp. 5–15, 24–27.

4. Perry G. E. Miller, "The Contribution of the Protestant Churches to Religious Liberty in Colonial America," *Church*

History, Vol. IV (1935), pp. 57–66, quoted by Mead (*Lively Experiment,* p. 19), who notes (*ibid.,* p. 36) as another authority for this view Anson Phelps Stokes's three-volume *Church and State in the United States.*

5. Padover (ed.), *The Complete Jefferson,* p. 676.

6. *Ibid.,* p. 538.

7. See the development in Mead, *Lively Experiment,* pp. 60–66.

8. See Richard E. Morgan, *The Politics of Religious Conflict* (Pegasus, 1968), pp. 20–22. Mead has also made this point ("The Fact of Pluralism," pp. 249–261) as well as Winthrop Hudson, *American Protestantism* (The University of Chicago Press, 1961), *passim.* The Episcopal Church, which has always had difficulty with the anti-authoritarian stance of other Protestant churches, is an obvious exception to this generalization.

9. Milton Himmelfarb, "Secular Society? A Jewish Perspective," in William G. McLoughlin and Robert N. Bellah (eds.), *Religion in America* (Beacon Press, Inc., 1968), p. 282.

10. Joseph L. Blau, "Alternatives Within Contemporary American Judaism," in *ibid.,* pp. 299–311.

11. John Courtney Murray, *We Hold These Truths* (Sheed & Ward, Inc., 1960), pp. 50, 54. This position has been ably argued by others, most notably Robert F. Drinan, *Religion, the Courts, and Public Policy* (McGraw-Hill Book Co., Inc., 1963).

12. Mead, *Lively Experiment,* p. 66.

13. De Tocqueville, *Democracy in America,* p. 312.

14. See Murray, *op. cit.* pp. 63–69.

15. Padover (ed.), *op. cit.,* p. 519.

16. James Madison, quoted in Sidney E. Mead, "Neither Church nor State: Reflections on James Madison's 'Line of Separation,' " *Journal of Church and State,* Vol. X (1968), p. 349.

17. Wilber G. Katz, "The Case for Religious Liberty," in John Cogley (ed.), *Religion in America* (Meridian Books, Inc., 1958), pp. 96–100.

18. Obviously this freedom is not unlimited, as the courts have decided when dealing with questions such as polygamy and snake handling. The juridical criterion for such limita-

tion is the extent to which a particular form of religious expression seriously violates either the public peace, or commonly accepted standards of public morality, or the rights of other citizens.

19. The language used by Justice Black in the famous *Everson* decision of 1947, for example, is quite different on the subject of "separation" from that of Justice Douglas five years later in *Zorach* v. *Clauson.* Black embraced the wall metaphor in all its impregnability, while Douglas, following Katz's line of reasoning, pointed out some of the bizarre consequences if the principle of strict separation were followed to its logical absurdity.

20. *Hudson County Water Co.* v. *McCarter,* 209 U.S. 349, 355 (1908).

21. Mead, "Neither Church nor State," p. 353.

22. This is the line that was drawn in *Everson* v. *Board of Education,* 330 U.S. 1 (1947). The law has remained at this line since then. The only question dividing the Justices in subsequent cases is that of deciding what precisely constitutes "aid." Thus a majority decided in 1948 that the use of public school property for religious instruction did constitute aid (*McCollum* v. *Board of Education,* 333 U.S. 203), while in 1952 another majority decided that releasing children for religious instruction away from school property did not constitute aid (*Zorach* v. *Clauson,* 343 U.S. 306). This reading of the No Establishment Clause has been opposed by an important group of constitutional critics, including Edwin N. Griswold, Mark De Wolfe Howe, and Edward S. Corwin. For their opinions, see Richard E. Morgan, *The Supreme Court and Religion* (The Free Press, 1972), pp. 183ff.

23. This argument has been advanced by many over the years. Confer, for example, Wilber G. Katz, "Religious Pluralism and the Supreme Court," in McLoughlin and Bellah (eds.), *op. cit.,* pp. 269–281.

24. *Zorach* v. *Clauson,* 343 U.S. at 313.

25. *Sherbert* v. *Verner,* 374 U.S., 398, 422 (1963).

26. Morgan, *Supreme Court and Religion,* p. 202.

27. See the provocative application of this sociological principle to Roman Catholic witness by Gregory Baum, "The Impact of Sociology on Catholic Theology," *Proceedings of*

the *Catholic Theological Society of America,* Vol. XXX (1975), pp. 1–29.

28. See the perceptive discussion of this recognition of mystery in *Religion and American Society,* a statement prepared by the Basic Issues Program of the Fund for the Republic and published in 1961 by the Center for the Study of Democratic Institutions at Santa Barbara.

29. Edward Schillebeeckx, *God—The Future of Man* (Sheed & Ward, Inc., 1968), pp. 191–199.

30. See the lengthy survey on world hunger in *The New York Times,* Jan. 25, 1976, and the special report, "Poor vs. Rich: A New Global Conflict," in *Time,* Dec. 2, 1975.

31. *Ibid.,* p. 40.

32. This has been the major theme of four papal encyclicals in recent years: John XXIII's *Mater et Magistra* and *Pacem in Terris,* and Paul VI's *Populorum progressio* and *Octogesima adveniens.*

33. See *Religion and American Society,* pp. 29–34.

34. See on this delicate issue the trenchant comments of Paul J. Weber, "Bishops in Politics: The Big Plunge," *America,* March 20, 1976.

35. *Religion and American Society,* p. 66.

CONCLUSION

1. Pierre Teilhard de Chardin, *The Future of Man* (Harper & Row, Publishers, Inc., 1964), p. 194.

2. The Yale Task Force on Population Ethics, "Moral Claims, Human Rights, and Population Policies," *Theological Studies,* Vol. XXXV (1974), p. 93. See the excellent treatment of the American constitutional tradition, pp. 92–96.

3. *Ibid.,* p. 95.

4. I am indebted for this example to the testimony of Margaret A. Farley of Yale University before the Subcommittee on Health of the House Ways and Means Committee on November 12, 1975. This was published in *Network Quarterly,* Vol. III (1975), pp. 1–4.

5. Robert Nozick, *Anarchy, State and Utopia* (Basic Books, Inc., 1974), pp. 32–33.

6. John Rawls, *A Theory of Justice* (Harvard University Press, 1971).

7. See the sensitive critique of the Warren Court in Alexander M. Bickel, *The Supreme Court and the Idea of Progress* (Harper & Row, Publishers, Inc., 1970).

8. Max Lerner, "The Constitution and the Court as Symbols," 46 *Yale Law Journal,* 1290 (1937).

9. In addition to Bickel's quiet warnings, see Nathan Glazer and Irving Kristol (eds.), *The American Commonwealth—1976* (Basic Books, Inc., 1976).

10. *Wyman* v. *James,* 400 U.S. 309, 347 (1970). (Dissenting opinion.)

11. Samuel D. Warren and Louis D. Brandeis, "The Right to Privacy," 4 *Harvard Law Review,* 193 (1890).

12. See the extensive treatment of the historical and case materials on the right in John A. Rohr, "Privacy: Law and Values," *Thought,* Vol. XLIX (1974), pp. 353–373.

13. B. F. Skinner, *Beyond Freedom and Dignity* (Bantam Books, Inc., 1972), p. 172.

14. Carl G. Jung, *The Undiscovered Self* (New American Library, Mentor Books, 1974), p. 119.

15. See the development of this insight in John C. Bennett, "America's Shift from Revolution to Counterrevolution," *The Christian Century,* June 9–16, 1976, pp. 561–564.